A Philosophical Daybook

A Philosophical Daybook

Post-Critical Investigations

WILLIAM H. POTEAT

University of Missouri Press
COLUMBIA AND LONDON

Library of Congress Cataloging-in-Publication Data
Poteat, William H.
    A philosophical daybook : post-critical investigations / William
H. Poteat.
    p.   cm.
    ISBN 0-8262-0748-0 (alk. paper)
    1. Philosophy. 2. Mind and body. 3. Poteat, William H.
Polanyian meditations. 4. Polanyi, Michael, 1891– . I. Title.
B945.P69P45   1990
191—dc20   90-34577
                                                                CIP

∞™ This paper meets the requirements of the
American National Standard for Permanence of Paper
for Printed Library Materials, Z39.48, 1984.

Designer: Liz Fett
Typesetter: Connell-Zeko Type & Graphics
Printer: Thomson-Shore, Inc.
Binder: Thomson-Shore, Inc.
Type face: Palatino

In memory of my father,
Edwin McNeill Poteat, Jr.
November 20, 1892–December 17, 1955

Contents

Acknowledgments

ROBERT J. BAIRD was an intimate and critical companion during the composing of these thoughts. I am more grateful for that fact even than for his contribution to the book itself.

It gives me pleasure publicly to thank John Berkman, Ian Carter, Murray Jardine, Araminta Johnston, and Elizabeth Newman for the time they gave to colloquies on the subjects of these *Investigations*.

To Ms. Christie Tyson, who received the crabbed pages of my notebook and gave me back the electronic miracle of printed pages—all done with great competence and good cheer—my heartfelt gratitude.

And how can one adequately thank a steadfast and inspiriting wife?

Walking is the gait of finitude.

————————— KIERKEGAARD

When Jogona had at last come to the end of his tale, and I had got it all down, I told him that I was now going to read it to him. He turned away from me while I was reading, as if to avoid all distractions.

But as I read out his own name, "And he sent for Jogona Kanyagga, who was his friend and who lived not far away," he swiftly turned his face to me, and gave me a great fierce flaming glance, so exuberant with laughter that it changed the old man into a boy, into the very symbol of youth. Again as I had finished the document and was reading out his name, where it figured as a verification below his thumbmark, the vital direct glance was repeated, this time deepened and calmed, with a new dignity.

Such a glance did Adam give the Lord when He formed him out of the dust, and breathed into his nostrils the breath of life, and man became a living soul. I had created him and shown him himself: Jogona Kanyagga of life everlasting. When I handed him the paper, he took it reverently and greedily, folded it up in a corner of his cloak and kept his hand upon it. He could not afford to lose it, for his soul was in it, and it was the proof of his existence. Here was something which Jogona Kanyagga had performed, and which would preserve his name for ever: the flesh was made word and dwelt among us full of grace and truth.

————————— ISAK DINESEN

If the true is what is grounded, then the ground is not *true*, nor yet false.

————————— WITTGENSTEIN

No word is natural upon utterance.

————————— ELON G. EIDENIER

A Philosophical Daybook

Introduction

IN NOVEMBER OF 1985 I received my first copy of *Polanyian Meditations: In Search of a Post-Critical Logic*, popped its plastic wrapper, and read it from cover to cover for the first time—ever. For two years prior to this I had been revising piecemeal, then editing copy, then proofing galleys and pages, then making indexes. By the end of this production process I had lost all sense of what the book was about, if indeed I'd ever had one. But I did most vividly recall how on a dreary morning in the spring of 1976 the book had, matter-of-factly— and certainly unaccompanied by any marks of supernatural sanction—simply appeared in my study and demanded to be written.

At the end of the prologue to the book with which I answered this vocation I had rhetorically asked: "What then are the central motifs that form the armature of these ever circling reflections? It is my view that rationality, that is, the 'hanging togetherness' of things for us, and logic, that is, the articulated form of the 'making sense' of things for us, are more deeply and ubiquitously, though inexplicitly, embedded in our ordinary thinking and doing than we are likely to notice. We fail to notice this because when called upon to reflect upon these facts we are likely to do so in the light of models— 'a picture held us captive'—formed by critical philosophy, beginning with Descartes, which increasingly took mathematics and formal logic to be the preeminent (and usually the only) paradigms of the 'hanging togetherness' of things and the 'making sense' of things. I argue therefore that contrary to the subtly pervasive 'picture' in the regnant Cartesianism of this culture that conceptually estranges thought about our minds from thought about our bodies, formalized rationality—mathematics and formal logic—derives from and remains parasitical upon the 'hanging togetherness' and 'sensemaking' of our integral mindbodily rootedness in the as yet unreflected world and in our unreflected 'thinkings' and doings in that world. This of course means that the mix among our uses of such concepts as 'reason,' 'logic,' 'body,' and 'mind,' to mention only some, will come to be drastically revised. For I claim that language—our first formal system—has the sinews of our bodies, which had them first; that the grammar, the syntax, the ingenuous choreography of our rhetorical engagement with the world, the meaning, the semantic and metaphorical intentionality of our language are pre-formed in that of our prelingual mindbodily being in the world, which is their condition of possibility. Mathematics is the ultimate achievement of our powers of abstraction and the medium of our ultimate access to the physical universe. It is therefore in it that our formalizing powers are conceptually most alienated from their somatic roots. Thus, when mathematics becomes our dominant even if not sole paradigm of reason, the 'picture' into which we easily fall to be held captive is that of a discarnate, i.e., the opposite of a mindbodily, being insofar as and when we are being rational. I contend therefore that when we speak of our world as an object or of our bodies as mere objects in the world, we use and can only use language generated out of a 'reality' more archaic to our history than and very different from 'mere objects in the world,' namely our lived and lively being in the world prior to speech which still bears traces of its primitive rootedness in this prelingual setting. The only thing I find surprising about this claim is that it somehow seems at once outrageous and self-evident."

In reading it straight through on this occasion I was astonished at its radicalism and at the richness of its implication. I thought: If this is the way things are, if the superordinate authority of the whole philosophical tradition is impeached, then absolutely everything will have to be rethought! Thank God, I will not live to do that. *Thank God*!

Until the moment of this reading I had felt, even as I sought to do the daily bidding of this uninvited guest, that my *real* life continued to be the same *old* life; that while acquiescing in the notices of my importunate visitor within the limits of five or six hours of writing every morning, I continued both to conduct my practical affairs and to transact my serious intellectual business in the same familiar currency. As I had said in the prologue of *Meditations*, its writing mainly required of me humility and obedience. The rest of the time, I had thought, was to be my own.

With this reading, however, a book that even in the writing had seemed an alien thing and that in the production process seemed hardly a book at all had, of a sudden, became something very different. It became, indeed, not a book of any sort, but a post-critical dwelling place, into which with all the rhetorical guile at my command I had sought to lure my readers, a place that I myself must now, once and for all, forswearing my "real life," begin permanently to inhabit.

As the meaning of this new environment gradually became clearer, the ironies of my place in it deepened. The very notion of *real life* became problematic. From the new dwelling place provided by *Polanyian Meditations* it now could be seen that what I had taken for "real life" was crusted over and skewed by acritically held images and values deriving from uncriticized Enlightenment criticism; and, at the same time, was discredited in principle as *real life*, that is, life that is potent with the unacknowledged configurations of meaning, coherence, order, and value, since its articulation was never the outcome of a skeptically induced inquiry—mandatory since the *Discourse* of Descartes—and therefore could not command the authority and epistemological weight—or even the interest—of the repertoire of the philosophical tradition. For me the old ground was increasingly undefendable and the new ground had yet to be taken.

What I began to do in 1987, about two weeks after turning in my fortieth and last set of year-end grades, was to sit down in my study every morning and, in a leather-bound book of blank pages, write down my reflections upon whatever philosophical perplexity was made to surface as I tried to learn what my way of thinking had become.

Sometimes the day's work amounted to a single grudging paragraph. On others it issued in a more or less self-contained étude of a thousand words, fitting neatly into the shape of the morning and the shape of the pages of my blank book. At other times the same perplexity was drawn out over many days, often followed by a break in the writing, but no gap in the processes of rumination.

It is conceivable that the reading of these pages will induce in you the clarification of certain philosophical opinions. For myself however they are an attempt to represent a certain new style of dwelling in one's mindbody in the world. I have therefore avoided editorial tampering with what was written in the longhand draft, hoping thereby to keep you as close as I found I had to keep myself to the concrete, agonistic, fully mindbodily activity of putting words upon the page in my own fair hand, which is, after all, one of the things that thinking is.

There is a stylistic price exacted by this, which I hope will not prove exorbitant. As I read over each day's installment in the original longhand draft, where the crises and risks of trying to rethink my own thought were vividly retained in the agitation in my hand and in its struggle with the limits of the pages, already bound in a book, the relentless reiteration of *mindbody* and its cognates gave little offense. After all, as I struggled to keep my footing while negotiating my way through the conceptual minefield of the philosophical tradition, as I had come to see it, it was necessary for me—and, I felt, for you, my reader, too—regularly to set foot on the solid ground upon which we jointly stand, namely, our convivial mindbodies, from which we could then once again sally forth.

Reading the same reflections from a typescript, the ingeminations of *mindbody*, now at some distance from the dangers that governed their original employment, at times became for me a weariness to the flesh. I considered heavily editing the typescript. It is certainly true that, as was pointed out by a sympathetic reader of even the longhand draft, we deal with one another not as mindbodies, but as *persons*. The argument, he suggested, should find some way of conveying this fact.

I finally decided to let the original stand for two reasons. First, and most important, excising *mindbody* from the original would serve further to alienate what you read from my own existential struggle to set my critical inheritance at a distance, which I wished to have transmuted into your existential struggle against *yours*. Second, yes, the use of *person* in our quotidian life is largely unproblematic. That is why, after a while, the soul cries out for it to take the place of *mindbody* in the text. Yet *person*, even though usually unequivocal in ordinary discourse, is, when it goes philosophical, very soon compromised by precisely the dualisms that I am seeking to expose.

I have therefore chosen to let things stand. As awkward as the reiteration of *mindbody* becomes in time, more is at stake than merely matters of style. A fundamental philosophical issue hangs in the balance: really, nothing less than the philosophical point of these *Investigations*.

You may feel, as I do, that the dualisms of this culture in general and the explicit philosophical doctrines of Descartes in particular have been polemicized about until we are left in a state of near stupefaction; that we can accordingly proceed as if these matters have been definitively settled at the philosophical level. After all, it requires no heroic feat to expose the Cartesian incoherences. Yet it persists, as I found in trying to address my own current philosophical perplexities from within the radical new perspective provided by *Polanyian Meditations*. Time and again, as I circled about my puzzlements, I found myself setting Cartesian traps for myself *in the very framing of my questions*. Cartesianism as an explicit philosophical doctrine is virtually without effect in this culture. It functions however at a tacit level like a repetition compulsion; it is ubiquitous and pervades the atmosphere of our life like chronic depression.

For it is in its impact upon philosophical anthropology, not only, not even primarily, as explicit doctrines, but as that which is implicated in *all* our thought and action, that it is most malign. Cartesianism, tacit and explicit, invites us to embrace a view of ourselves in the universe which seduces us with the promise of Godlike power, and thereby separates us from our true ground and humanity. Nowhere is this malignity so much in evidence as in those forms of humanistic endeavor and scholarship—the very phrase, "*humanistic endeavor*," is itself a cry of despair—where the putative import of scientism is taken with utter uncritical seriousness; whereas it is paid little mind in science. Nihilism, though lethal, is embraced as a form of honesty that will save us.

It will be immediately obvious that this is no work of scholarship. The degree and nature of one's fealty toward the bearers of one's tradition very much depend upon the range at which one needs at once to behold and be beholden to them; and that is dictated by the nature of the business at hand. The Immanuel Kant of these reflections, for example, is not the provocation of some carefully defended historical assessment. For me he has been my tempter and the provocateur of my imagination—but always at a distance.

What I aspire to for you is the same thing I have sought for myself: growing consolidation in a post-critical mode of mindbodily being through the step-by-step and painstaking examination of some old philosophical puzzles, reimagined and rearticulated, until they are transformed into the commonplaces of a new form of *real life*—so that, for example, we will be able, under the vault of heaven, to say with no tinge of self-consciousness what we are, in any case, ingenuously *inclined* to say: "The heavens declare the glory of God and the firmament showeth his handiwork."

In our culture the time for relocating the axis of our existence is very late; perhaps it has already passed. It is still possible, nonetheless, for us to remain steadfast at our posts.

Investigations

When (how) does the distinction between direct and figurative language arise? Does not this very question about the force of different forms of discourse presuppose that the only (principal) function of language is the making of assertions? Or can we issue commands, offer prayers, utter blessings, solemnize marriages *figuratively*. I might observe that "give us this day our daily bread" is the use of a *figure* inasmuch as this is not, in the setting of the Lord's Prayer, a *literal* petition for bread on the table. But how do we apply the literal/figurative distinction here? When I say the words "give us this day . . ." is there anything equivocal in my use; do they have less force than if they were taken to mean (literally?) "Bread on the table, please"?

But what would the *figurative* solemnization of a marriage be? And could this not occur even with all the felicities (Austin) provided? Would we say, "Well, all of the participants didn't mean what they said and did *literally*." Or is it rather that they *really, fully, unequivocally* meant what they said and did, only differently? Is *Hamlet* the figurative representation of an actual (historical) Prince of Denmark?

Well, there are analogies among the imaginary/real, fiction/history, figurative/direct, metaphorical/literal, mythos/logos distinctions. And underlying these there seems to be the acceptance of the fact that we dwell in the first member of each of these binary pairs differently from the way we dwell in the second; and that even if it is perhaps inevitable that we will occasionally dwell in the first, we ought and can only be serious about dwelling in the second. Yet is not having and being in a world precisely to dwell alternately and

7

often richly simultaneously, but never less than *fully*, in both terms of each of these pairs? Indeed, is not the tension among these pairs in which we simultaneously dwell the very source of our existential tonus, our mindbodily oriented presence.

Even so, our ingenuous and acritical confidence in the integrity of the world so appropriated (a confidence deriving from the fact that at any given moment all of the forms of the real in their richly overdetermined layers cohere in our lively mindbodily tonus) is in jeopardy to the supposition that only that is *really* real which is the *terminus ad quem*, quite narrowly construed, of a name-relation theory of meaning.

Is there something peculiarly odd about wanting to imagine a figurative solemnization of marriage, burial of the dead? If so, why?

What I have in mind here is the question of the status of the ceremony *as a whole* in contrast to the (possibly) figurative language of some (or all, even) of its constituent linguistic parts. Consider the enormous logical complexity of the Apostle's Creed when viewed apart from its *use*.

6/17/87

We use language (words) in ways that we take and that are taken by others to be figurative. We remark them by expressions like: "So to speak, as it were; etc." Can our gestures ever be indirect, figurative? Or do they always mean just what they mean and not something else?

I think that some of the time when we say of what we say, "so to speak, as it were," we are signaling to our hearers—gratuitously, I think—that we mean these words in one way and not in some other; as if we are flagging the grammar of our expression. I say that saying "so to speak" is a gratuitous reflection upon the grammar of our usage because our hearers are hardly ever misled when we omit this warning.

Imperiously, I say to you: "Shut the door." You snap to attention and salute. This leads me to apologize. Your action, we might say, is an ironical comment upon my tone of "command." How would the situation be different, if I were your commanding officer and we were in uniform? Certainly the salute in the two cases has a different meaning, a different force. But we wouldn't be inclined to think that the salute in the first case is figurative or indirect or has only a derivative force, whereas in the second it is literal or direct or somehow bedrock.

Yet, why am I inclined to say of some of my expressions things like "as it were," "so to speak," "in a manner of speaking"? Those qualifications suggest that this particular use of language is of an equivocal sort, not fully serious, possessing only a secondary force. But compared to what? And why *that* paradigm?

When I say "So to speak . . ." I seem to be expressing the fact of my tacit recognition of many different possible layers of meaning in an expression, of the surplus of meaning in language. But recognizing this, why do I feel impelled to issue a *caveat* about one of my expressions? Is it because as a speaker I want to impart an authority and force to *some* of my words which I wish to be withheld from others of them? But is this true? Do I not accord authority and force to the words segregated by "so to speak," only a different authority and force? After all, I *do* asseverate the segregated words; and what do I mean by "different authority" here?

Often, perhaps when we are speaking quite ingenuously and without self-consciousness, we omit this warning. We say "The poor man was at the end of his rope" or "I was up to my ass in alligators" and do not think to ask about the authority and force of this language. What is it that brings us ever to wonder this? What is the role in our speech practice of "so to speak" and "as it were"? Well, for one thing to say "as it were," "so to speak" is to express our appreciation of the irony of our relation to language.

Is the coming of literacy a clue here? We are apt (are we not) to say "as it were" when our speech is shot through with a certain self-consciousness, reflexivity. Do not the sophists with *politiké techné* and Socrates with his "know thyself" follow upon the self-consciousness educed by literacy?

6/18/87

Suppose that you chance to hear a congregation of people utter in unison the words "Give us this day our daily bread"—surrounded by the stage setting of worship, preceded and followed by the usual words of the Lord's Prayer. Being a modern person, what will you make of this? And let us stipulate that for you the matter of acquiring bread has to do either with obtaining the ingredients and baking it for yourself or saying to the clerk in the bakery shop, "Here's my money. Give me my daily bread"—or something like these two cases. Acquiring and being able to eat one's daily bread is serious business; next to breathing itself, the most serious of all. The *essentials* of it are to be found in the above two sorts of cases—however otherwise adorned these activities may be. But what are we to make of these people on their knees, saying aloud, it appears, to no one in particular, and certainly to no bakery shop clerk: "Give us this day our daily bread." If we are complacent, we will say that these people are confused or benighted. They *think* they are (literally?) asking for bread when they could not be. If we are *not* complacent, we might suppose that their language bears in some figurative way upon *the literal* state of affairs described in terms of our above two cases—in suggesting which we are not forgetting that "give me my daily bread" spoken to the bakery clerk is direct, serious, and more likely to be efficacious than the "figurative" language of those on their knees. The literal/figurative distinction still has authority over us. What is literal and direct is what is serious and real; all the rest of our talk is, however pleasing and even irresistible, secondary or tertiary. Nevertheless, if we are particularly acute, we may come to see that distinguishing between shopping for bread and "praying for bread" by invoking the literal/figurative distinction sheds no light. It only reinforces our modernist prejudice. The weight and force of the words "Give us this day our daily bread," uttered in the setting of prayer, are exactly what they are and not some other thing: As direct and unequivocal as can be, which no translation can improve or further legitimize. These words are among those that give form to the world in which I live.

6/19/87

At any given moment we have no doubt that our world has a future. "Having no such doubt" is indeed *the very condition* of my referring to "any given moment." Yet what is its status? Is it real, imaginary, fictive? We wonder about this question *in this way* because of our belief that the past has a reality insofar as we can *recount it in words* and the future can be the subject of a possible story. Is there not a sense in which the future is quite as real—not a fiction—as the past. It's just different. We can misjudge it in different ways from our misjudgments about the past. What does it mean to talk of misjudgments here. What is the underlying picture of these statements? Our *de facto unreflected* mindbodily orientation to and ensconcement *in* the past and the future is ignored in this picture.

6/20/87

At any given moment our lively mindbodies retrotend our worldly past as a *present* reality and pretend our worldly future as a *present* reality; and when we speak of them—whether in language which refers to past particular actualities and future particular possibilities or alternatively in quite general terms—we refer to them as *present* realities, as real as can be. In this sense the past is not past and the future not future. Things will appear quite different, if I reflect upon these matters from within the theater of solitude situated in a slice of dead (visual) space. Then I shall imagine the past as no longer and the future as not yet and will suppose that, since in the present moment (an atemporal "moment" in a dead slice of visual space) they do not exist, references to them are problematical, i.e., cannot be *direct*, though, of course, problematical in different ways. Obviously the *possible* act of tomorrow to which I refer by saying "Tomorrow I shall X" has a different reality than the *actual* act of yesterday to which I refer by saying "Yesterday I Y'ed." Perhaps it does not seem so odd to say that yesterday's actuality is a *present* actuality in the ligatures of the overdetermined meanings which compose my present mindbodily being. It *seems* more problematical however to say that for my temporally distended mindbody in the present tomorrow's *possibility*—whether we think of this in specific or not so specific terms—is a *present actuality*. In other words the future *already is* as either the specific or general pretensions of my tonic mindbody. There is, then, nothing of the *as if . . .* about our references to the future, no want of an "ontological" ground for it; even if that ground is different from my retrotended *past* acts in the present.

6/22/87

The temptation to give in to the visualist pictures that we both *have* and are *in the midst of* which are parts of the stage setting of the use in our philosophical puzzling of 'past', 'future', 'before', 'after', etc., is all but irresistible. In thinking of a succession of musical notes I am very likely to imagine at a given "moment" that the notes I have heard are "back there" and the notes I anticipate hearing are "up ahead," as they would appear within the (visual) space of the musical score. The force of 'past' in this theater of reflection is "back there" or "over there" in relation to where I now stand in (visual) space, which is of course the present; the force of 'future' is "up ahead" in (visual) space. In the setting of *this* theater of reflection where 'past' and 'future' have this use and force it is nonsensical to say, as above, that "the past is not past and the future not future." This statement is an oblique statement about a different way to talk about time.

If however I retain my stand within my existentially actual mindbody that is at every moment caught up in the *always present* pretensions and retrotensions of time, for whom indeed to *exist in a moment* is precisely to be so caught up, then my reflections will be taking place in a quite different theater. 'Past' and 'future' will have a different use. There will continue to be perplexities about the legitimation of claims about past events and future events. But it will no longer be necessary to wonder whether there could be any present reality upon which allusion to the future can bear in the present. A better way to put this is to say that our matter-of-fact references to the past and to the future—even if only to the moment just "past" or the "moment" we immediately anticipate—derive their authority and indubitability from their grounding in our primitive worldliness prior to our alienation from it in reflection. It is in this primitive worldliness that the weight and authority of myth are founded. In our artless uses of the past and future tenses in ordinary speech, there is not the slightest doubt betrayed, since none is felt, that what we say bears upon a real and integral world—one whose past and future are present as we speak.

6/23/87

Earlier I have spoken of the analogies among the imaginary/real, fiction/history, figurative/direct, metaphorical/literal, mythos/logos distinctions and conclude that the tension between each member of these binary pairs in which we richly simultaneously dwell is the source of our existential tonus, our mindbodily oriented presence; and that at any given moment all of the forms of the real in their richly overdetermined layers cohere in our mindbodies. Now, does saying this commit me to some form of idealism? How does this question about idealism/realism get raised? Clearly these are the standard questions of the philosophic tradition; but how did they get *there*? Why is it I find the suggestion that I am some kind of idealist vaguely disconcerting? What is it I *deeply* believe that does not comport with being an idealist? The premises are offensive to me in some profound way.

First, a premise of idealism is a belief in the conceivability of (let us take Berkeley, for example) sensations, ideas, notions as if they were given *in themselves*, independent of the distentions of time, disembrangled by means of reflection from the mindbodily actuality of the mindbodily thinker. The theater of reflection in which they appear is really a fantasy of (visual) space, with all the limitations thereof. The mindbody from which issue our feats of reflection and their fruits—articulated percepts and concepts—is systematically overlooked while its fruits are given a privileged status as real. [The kind of indubitability that the world has and that is supposed by Berkeley to be supplied by God is in fact supplied by my mindbody.]* Thus, to *be* is to have that kind of reality which a perception is depicted as having, *thus described*. All the choirs of heaven and all the furniture of earth are exactly as we know them to be in our perceptions, only these perceptions are *depicted* as being autonomous, independent of because abstracted from our mindbodily existence. Indeed, even our "bodies" are what we *perceive* them to be in the above sense of 'perceive'; and to these we have no preperceptual (as this is described above) access as the touchstone of a "mind-*independent*" reality (as this is understood in the above description). If percepts and concepts are seen to be inextricably and irreducibly implicated with our motility, sentience, and orientation in the world as mindbodies, then the ground upon which the idealism/realism opposition gets its traction is taken away.

How then do we use the word 'real'? I will take to be real, *we* will convivially take to be real, the world to which we find ourselves oriented through all of the modalities of our mindbodily being in which it coheres. Perhaps, then, the question "Is this real?" is not the question—or not often the question—"Does this have any standing in the (real?) world?" but, "What *kind of* standing does it have?" "If we take X to be our paradigm for the real, is *this* real?" "Is the reality of this X that we are talking about the same sort as or different from the reality of this Y?" When we use the expression 'real world' we are almost certain to buy into the regnant paradigm for this in the philosophic tradition.

6/24/87

So long as *I* take my stand within my tonic mindbodily being, sentient and oriented in my as-yet-unreflected primitive world-

[* All material within brackets was interpolated in the typescript.]

liness; so long as *we* mutually and convivially stand in this primitive worldliness; the weight and value in this world (which coheres in our lively, intentional, convivial mindbodies), of what from time to time we find it, for certain critical purposes, convenient to call direct or figurative discourse, real/imaginary, history/fiction, literal/metaphorical, logos/mythos, will here have a very different sense.

Often these distinctions will serve as the means of identifying the grammar of the discourse just now in use in a given feat of reflection; no longer as the means for ranking the truth-bearing powers of different modes of discourse.

Sometimes when I say to you, "So and so, *as it were* . . ."—on some occasion when it is conceivable that without this warning you might be misled, and these are very rare—I am signaling that the words which precede "as it were" are figurative *in relation to what follows*. When I, relying upon the distinction between history and fiction, say to you, "Let me tell you a true story," in this culture I am taken to mean a story such as would be reported in the *New York Times*, sworn to under oath as having happened, etc. Does Shakespeare's *Hamlet* embody a true story? Yes! But of that other sort. Both the above "true" story and *Hamlet* insofar as they equally cohere in our intentional and convivial mindbodies and insofar as we dwell *in* them, even in our ingenuous worldliness, enjoy equal standing in the fabric of the world.

If I were to say, "According to what I've said above, you see, even the imaginary is real," you might be inclined to say: "Well, yes, I suppose there is a sense in which you could say that. But the 'imaginary', of course, is 'real' only in a weak, derived, metaphorical—merely psychological—sense." And I reply: "No. You don't get it at all. What is *imagined* is as *real*, as *potent*, *as intractable* as can be. Its reality, potency, and intractability are those of the *imaginary* rather than those of a different sort, associated with what you think of as the paradigm of real. Furthermore, its jurisdiction is not the unreliable and overfecund psyche. To use 'psychological' as you have is to suggest the merely 'mental'." [Here, unsure of my footing, that is, estranged from my mindbodily self as the center from which all of my world-forming pretensions radiate, I am not attending to how we actually use 'imaginary' and 'real' in ordinary discourses. Instead, I am choosing sides between them on the basis of the paradigms of the philosophical tradition.] The imagination is generated out of our lively, sentient, motile, and oriented mindbodies in their primitive worldliness, pretending their meanings, logos, and order;

continually retrotending the mindbodies whose very issue they are. To dwell in the imaginary is therefore not to dwell in the "mind" or "consciousness" or "just in your head." It is to dwell in one of the forms taken by our mindbodily life, itself grounded in the real, and ceaselessly testifying to this ground.

Only a philosopher would have to make so obvious a point so ponderously, for only a philosopher would have to go so strenuously against his cultivated impulses in order to recover his senses. Most of the time we use "as it were" and "so to speak" out of sheer spontaneous poetic delight in the intersecting logics of the richly overdetermined discourse—what critics make much of as irony and metonymy—of our most ordinary talk.

As epistemologists we have no reason to favor one physiology or psychology of perception over another. They are all equally irrelevant to a truly radical *epistemological* concern with perception. The dangers of using 'epistemology' here—all the bad dualistic company it keeps.

6/26/87

What is the world in which we "live and move and have our being"? The Enlightenment has inclined us to imagine ourselves as being independent of, disentangled from, the world which is depicted as over against us, as an object of lucid reflection; and to imagine *ourselves* as yet other objects for thought which can then be shown to participate in this world (as described) as knowers and doers (as described). The world and humankind that can appear in this kind of reflection and that can be seen as related to one another as they are in this kind of reflection are the *real* world and humankind. What does *not* appear here—which is to say the rich tapestry of meanings that form the background and horizons of our being as knowers and doers—does not exist, or does not *really* exist, according to this view.

When, from within this theater of reflection, we take up the questions concerning the literal and metaphorical, history vs. fiction or logos vs. mythos—distinctions whose tacit forms *issue* in reflection and whose explicit forms *appear* only there [or more exactly, *tacit* distinctions rooted in the as-yet-unreflected appreciations by our mindbodies of the ironies already given within the fabric of our primitive worldliness and *explicit* distinctions that are their issue in reflection]—we shall be undertaking to assign the weight and authority of each of the members of these binary pairs as these are assessed in the setting of the above picture of the world, of humankind and of the relation between them. We undertake, in short, to define the role in the articulation of the world of the literal vs. the metaphorical, of history vs. fiction, of logos vs. mythos; to remark the analogies and disanalogies between each of the members of these binary pairs, and on this basis to evaluate and characterize the nature of their truth-bearing power. Given this theater of reflection, the game is, of course, rigged in favor of the literal, of history, of logos. Any derivative truth-bearing power that the second member of each binary pair is thought to have is but a function of its analogies with the first member of each pair.

We are then handed this world and humankind in it that has been abstracted piece by piece from our primitive worldliness by feats of reflection, and then has been laboriously reassembled by yet further such feats, and are told that this is the *real* world.

Now, the fact is, *this is a real world*, even though almost the only time we spend in it is when we are engaged in *reflection* about the nature of things. But it is a secondary world, a derivative one, drawn by reflection from reflection's own roots in our motile, sentient, oriented, and intentional mindbodies; an often useful object of thought for all manner of intellectual purposes; and only dangerous to humankind when this derivative world is taken, by reason of its assumed primacy, to be the preferred, if indeed not the only, setting within which to frame the questions of philosophical anthropology; to be primary; and when, as has happened in modernity, its images enter and come to form our "common sense."

And what then is the world in which we "live and move and have our being"? It is the progeny of all of the world-forming powers of our intentional mindbodily beings—from our breathing in and breathing out, to the styles of our gaits, to the rhythm and timbre of our speech, to our song and dance, to all of our ordinary knowings and doings, to our practice of mathematical heuristics etc., with no *in principle* assignment of special privilege and authority, where world-formation is concerned, to any one of these powers. In the words that I wrote above, "What is *imagined* is as *real*, as *potent*, as *intractable* as can be," I have not succeeded in stating clearly how it is that I wish differently to think about imagination. These words have one uncontroversial meaning for the Enlightenment philosopher, a different one for me in the setting of the different theater of my reflection sketched out immediately above. Between the two views there lies a revolution.

6/27/87

When actors play upon the stage, do they experience what they do and say and the setting in which they find themselves as imaginary? The world on the stage may not be experienced as of the same sort as that beyond the footlights. But I do not believe it is a diminished reality. I can tell the difference between my "real" anger and the feigned anger that my role in the play calls for, else I should become insane. But in the context where anger is feigned it is as unequivocal as I am capable of making it, subject to the grammar of the play. Notice how actors, in a twinkling of an eye, become other people, with faces we have not seen before, the instant the curtain call is taken. Occasionally one of the company, under the burden of his or her role, doesn't quite make it back into the "real" world in time. He or she still looks familiar. This only underscores my point. There is no space for skepticism to insert itself between me and my feigned anger; at least none does insert itself. [The relation between "real" and "feigned" anger is far more complex than I have suggested here.]

6/29/87

What is the role in the formation of the world in which we live and move and have our being of our kneeling together and saying: "Give us this day our daily bread"? Of *my* kneeling alone and saying this?

Sometimes we make a commonsensical distinction between an event or act and the mere "ritual" that surrounds it, even if this is accomplished by nothing more explicit than a pejorative reference to the latter. Is this not part of our Enlightened suspicion of (mere) ceremony and ritual—the meaningless residues of a tradition that we wish to abandon. There is no doubt that these "trappings," as we are tempted to call them, come to lose all authority, are emptied of meaning and come to veil reality from us—"Wittgenstein's Vienna," for example. But this fact about the loss of meaning in human institutions which revolutions herald is seriously misrepresented by the ideologues of revolution. From the standpoint of their ideology it is thought to be easy to distinguish between the perennial springs of human action and its accreted, historically parochial accoutrements. The new ideology, focusing upon what it takes to be the fundamentals of human action—the *real thing*, in short—is able to isolate for attack all that can, from this perspective, be seen as meretricious, deliberately deceitful, or without meaning.

As they busily set about beginning history *de novo* by uprooting mythos and exposing the emptiness of ritual, the ideologues are fashioning a new mythos, *necessarily* attended by its emerging new ritual. [This glib distinction between mythos and its ritual betrays my captivity to an Enlightened way of conceiving of their relation.] And as this usually takes place all unwittingly, the relation between ritual and human action is left unexamined; or more accurately, the question as to the nature of human action is taken to have been already answered—by the new myth.

This certainly is the legacy of the *philosophes* of our Enlightenment. When Comte proposed to found the institutions of a religion of humanity, the irony was lost on him that it had already been "founded" in the only place where religion could be, namely, in the unreflected depths of European life.

The pejoration that so often rules our use of 'ritual', 'ceremony', 'rite' has its roots in this historical experience and its mythology. And this latter also afflicts us with a dualism of acts or events, on one hand, and their putatively merely attendant rituals, on the other. We take it for granted that we know where the incision goes. Let us examine one kind of case.

6/30/87

What is it to bat a baseball? Let us assume I've been instructed to "hit away"; nothing tricky, no bunt, no sacrifice fly, no hit and run, no squeeze play, etc. What is it for me to bat a baseball? It is to bring the fat part of the bat to bear upon a baseball flying toward home plate at between 80 and 90 miles an hour while I stand in the batter's box. This might be said to be the "basic thing," a "physical" act the telos of which is interrupting the flight of the ball in such a way as at least to get safely to first base. It is this telos that enables me to define what constitutes the "basic thing." It is easy enough to imagine a context in which this would be a quite satisfactory answer to the question, What is it to bat a baseball? And the fact that I have severely abstracted the terms of the answer from the particularities of my act of entering the batter's box in an actual game situation, etc., etc., makes my answer appropriate to the context of the question and also renders my identification of the "basic thing" philosophically harmless. Armed with such an account we would perhaps be inclined to say that swinging the bat through an arc that will bring the fat part into contact with the ball is the "basic thing" in batting; all of the other accompaniments—the swinging of two or three bats as you walk from dugout to on-deck circle, kneeling in a certain way while waiting, adjusting your socks and pants, tugging at the bill of your cap, knocking the mud—real or (usually) imagined—from your cleats with your bat, squaring yourself in the batter's box and striking the opposite side of home plate, etc., etc.—are secondary or tertiary to the "basic thing." As cultural anthropologists with these premises, we might be inclined to think that striking the ball is here surrounded by a good deal of rich and complex ritual behavior which has no discernible logical connection with the telos of this act and is therefore just inexplicable. Or if we were less doctrinaire, we might concede that this particular ritual behavior does have the effect of relieving muscular tension and mastering anxiety. Now "tension" and "anxiety" become natural ingredients in a broadened conception of the "basic thing." [Or is thought by the natives to be designed to invoke the favor of the Gods.]

What changes however if we say that batting a baseball is the act of achieving the optimum degree of coherent mindbodily motility, sentience, and orientation in the world—*of a particular sort*; that is to say, of the "baseball-batting-sort"—a matter of knowing where and how to place yourself in the world and then placing yourself there?

Well, our complacency about what is the "basic thing" and what the secondary and tertiary ritual accompaniments are and where the incision goes will be severely shaken. Swinging three bats and clearing your cleats, like swinging the bat at a pitched ball, are equally parts of the "basic thing."

The techniques for the "release of muscular tension" and the "mastery of anxiety" will still be required; only now they will have their significance as elements—and in no way privileged elements—in our account of the feat of placing oneself in the world with optimum coherence in a baseball-batting-way.

Is it an exaggeration to say that *everything we do*—except things that we do by accident—whether it is done in solitude or convivially, from breathing in a certain way to acts of speculation, is done to enable us to achieve and maintain our optimum mindbodily coherence with the world? There is a multitude of ways for distinguishing one set of things we do from another set—each according to the job that needs to be done. The distinction between the "basic thing" and ritual is but one such. And our view of where the incision goes is a part of our Enlightenment dogma that must be challenged.

7/1/87

A certain degree of reflection often enters into the flow of my, as I might call it, "purely" practical activity. As I write on this white page with my pen the words do not appear there as if this is the work of a machine. I am about to write the word *conceive* and *there is a sense in which* I "remember" the spelling rule about I before E except after C as I "approach" the word. By contrast, in writing the words *there is a sense in which*, I "reflect" upon no spelling rules. The words flow uninhibited by reflection from the tip of my pen.

I sit and puzzle over the relation between action and reflection, and over why my written words do not seem to appear on the page as if they are the work of a machine. I look out the window; I write, "I look out the window," and stop. Glancing about, I spy an uncrossed "t" in the paragraph above and cross it. I blow into my fist. I reread the two preceding sentences—"Let's see, where am I," I half-think. I now vaguely remember that this puzzle was already beginning to take form two hours ago on my morning jog, just as I took a left off Dover Road onto Surrey. My present recollection of my puzzlement is stamped with the local colors of the specific place I was when it first announced itself: the sprinklers blasting away, forming a rainbow on the 6th green, the treacherous footing in loose gravel at the turn onto Surrey.

All of this—and of course much more, if I chose here to give it some kind of explicit standing—seems (here a long interruption as I "search"—where?—for the word that actually embodies the sense of the immediately above as I already, but still elusively, have it in my oriented mindbody, seeking fuller, more complete orientation) to be ligated by the logos that enforms my lively motile, sentient, oriented mindbody and courses through all of the senses, images, half-thoughts, thoughts, perceptions, puzzlements half-formed, and gross bodily movements through a landscape of events to seek a resolution of my thinking/doing in the apposite words taking form on this page. It is because thinking/writing involves all of this—and more—that it could not be done by a machine. Throughout all of this effort at expressing ideas in written words, I have been reiterating my orientation to the *ur*world as a condition of this ratiocination.

7/2/87

No doubt an actor's relation to the role he is playing on the stage is as complex and many-layered as my relation to myself in my acts of

presenting myself in the world. There are no doubt analogies between the relations of "acting" and reflecting upon "acting" and
those of acting and reflecting upon it. What I've said above about
the relation between me and my feigned anger is doubtless sometimes true on the stage. But not always; perhaps for an excellent
actor rarely so. This of course will depend on the school of acting to
which he subscribes. Whatever the case, the issue of reality and
realities is not less complex than the subtle play that is manifest in
this case among the different modalities of our appearance in the
world.

7/8/87

My dispute with sociology, say, insofar as I have one, is over philosophical anthropology. *Polanyian Meditations* is a systematic and radical rejection of the modern philosophic tradition—even of the *whole*
tradition of philosophy as such—insofar as it embodies and
expresses an anthropology—and of course from the perspective of
Polanyian Meditations, be the philosophy ever so abstract (a "scientific" epistemology, say), it *necessarily* entails an implicit view of man
in the world. The reason for this entailment lies of course in the fact
that the theater in which reflection is conceived to take place dis-
poses us toward a certain view of ourselves in relation to the objects
of reflection. Even if this theater is always (or usually) at reflection's
back, it is decisive for the philosophic agenda that reflection sets for
itself, as Descartes' paradigmatic modern theater of solitude is for
our agenda.

When someone says, "Language is the instrument of both our
individuation and our socialization," we can immediately see how
there is an implicit anthropology at work in this remark because of
the theater of solitude in which it is conceived. For here it is assumed that individuation begins when I acquire a native language—
I can now use 'I' and 'me'—and socialization begins when I can use
'we' and 'us'. Of course, to learn the use of *I*, to learn to *use* it, I must
learn simultaneously to use *we*. Individuation and socialization occur in the selfsame moment. The perspective implicit in this framing of the question is that of a mature user of a language who has a
lucid command of its resources in a position of detachment from
any actual acts of speech. From this view of language, we then
imagine that the preverbal child is given an instrument such as only
a mature and skillful speaker explicitly possesses, discovers that he

is an individual among others because he understands the grammar of the personal pronouns in the singular and plural in the way that a grammarian and linguist would. Whereas, of course, language is at once the *issue of* and is *grounded in* all of the preverbal processes of individuation already at work in us, and the instrument of our further, verbal "individuation" and "socialization." Trying to think *radically* about individuation and socialization in the abstract is exactly parallel to thinking about the grammar of 'I' abstracted from the grammar of 'We'. In other words, the theater of solitude dictates one way of understanding the grammar of 'individual', 'social', 'language'; the alternative one of *Polanyian Meditations* dictates another. The result is two different philosophical anthropologies.

7/9/87

In calling this a difference between anthropologies I may seem to be making a weak case, since philosophical anthropology may appear to be less than the bedrock of a philosophical position. It is true of course that the meaning of the words *philosophical anthropology* in the modern philosophical tradition is one thing, quite something else in the new view of things set forth in *Polanyian Meditations*. In the tradition philosophical anthropology is one focus of inquiry alongside others—epistemology, ontology, metaphysics, ethics, etc.— all mutually implicative, all sharing a commitment to a problematic rooted in the subject-object dichotomy, sustained by the theater of solitude. By contrast, the import of *Polanyian Meditations* is that this dichotomy is not radical but derived; that even reflection arises from, depends upon, and continuously retrotends our lively mindbodies: sentient, motile, and oriented in their world, antecedent to but also contemporaneous with this reflectively generated dichotomy. This mindbodily anthropological fact is bedrock for *P.M.*; and from the perspective of *P.M.* this datum is the *de facto* bedrock of *all* philosophies, whatever may be their *de jure* demurrers.

8/10/87

Critics therefore who have charged *P.M.* with having scanted the dimension of the "social" bring to bear upon it a concept the force of which is systematically under radical transformation there. The "possibility of sociality" is a problematic peculiar to the modernist theater of solitude, since the isolated *cogito* is the given certainty and the bonds of its relation to others are required to be explicitly established—whether the individual is conceived to be a self amid other selves, an atom falling with other atoms through space by chance, a windowless monad among windowless monads, etc. The various ingenious devices for overcoming the presumed bedrock, inherent ontological opposition between centered selfhood and the multitude of others over against it, gain their traction and derive their plausibility from the theater of reflection within which they are worked through. For *Polanyian Meditations*, on the contrary, it is our integral sentient, oriented, motile mindbodies, bonded in their efferent intentions to a world prior to reflection, which are the *radical* given, from within which all opposition and otheration derive, in which they remain rooted—whether this be self-other, here/now-there/then, efferent-afferent, pretension-retrotension, I/me-we/us, or most abstractly, *this* atom-all those other atoms. In other words self and other, I and you, solitude and society, individuation and socialization have at bedrock the same provenance for *P.M.* This is why they are mutually implicative for reflection.

The Frankfurt school—Marxist criticism in general—can be judged on its merits on its own terms for its heuristic value. From the perspective of *P.M.* it must be judged to be an untenable, implicit philosophical anthropology. How so? No critical posture is conceivable which does not imply a view of where and how man stands vis-à-vis the objects of his criticism. That implied in the Frankfort school is not, as philosophical anthropology, truly radical.

8/12/87

What does it mean to speak of this, or any school of criticism, as "philosophical anthropology"; and to characterize it as less than truly radical?

8/13/87

In a literate culture it is natural to imagine that words and concepts have an existence independent of the time of our mindbodies because as written they are contemporaneous in a dead slice of (visual) space and are connected to one another by modes inherent in and exclusive to this medium. Their "meanings" and the mutual implicativeness of their "meanings" as words—their logos—come to be imagined to inhere in and to *consist* in their static juxtaposition in visual space. This image becomes superordinate over the melodic connectedness of spoken words in time. Our picture of words is drawn from literacy.

One of the things that we discover when we attend with great care to the process by which thought makes its way onto the page is that it is not at all the exfoliation of a series of "intellectual," "conceptual," verbal connections—understanding these notions as they are used in the philosophical tradition—that possess a logic intrinsic to themselves alone and have a strictly *extrinsic and contingent* connection to the "physical" acts involved in writing—as for example we might think of the computer's program as the sum of all of its tokens and terms, subject to its grammar, having an integrity in itself as software, quite apart from its contingent relation to the mainframe which will print out its "findings" on demand. This indeed tends—and more and more so—to be the model in terms of which we think of thinking. [Indeed, a computer program is without remainder an embodiment of thought as *fait accompli* and tells us nothing about thinking except its consummation.] This may be a useful and, under strict supervision, a benign model for depicting articulated thought as *fait accompli*. It has however no bearing whatever upon thought as an emergent of my mindbodily activity, issuing at last in intelligible words upon a page.

As, in writing, I grope toward the articulation of half-formed ideas and am therefore coming to focus upon the verbal resources that are *indeed* at hand—*at hand* since "groping" is quite exactly a reaching out in order to *bring to* hand; to bring from out of the background and, in the logos of my integral mindbody, into the consenter of this pneumocarnal hand that writes the emerging words upon the page—I am continually making reference to my circumambient *ur*world by seeing and hearing there what there is to see and hear; by my contemporaneous movings, gesturings, and focusings; by my remembered scenes, sounds, and images; by my prospective fantasies; by my efferent pretensions and afferent retrotensions. Because of our literacy, because the agonizing *process* of thinking culminates in a static and "permanent" embodiment, we are led to imagine that it was always accomplished, "there," in the "computer program" just waiting for us to "print it out." As we've seen above, thinking is quite as inextricably incarnate and local as everything else we do. It was Cartesianism and its theater of the solitary ego that caused us to suppose otherwise. "Mentalism" is a product of literacy.

8/14/87

These claims are rendered still more plausible if we consider another phenomenon.

When I reread some of these notes several weeks after they were written, I do not understand them—even though I can remember that at the time of writing I was satisfied with their intelligibility, even to another reader. Yet now I have to read them over repeatedly and puzzle and ponder—until finally they clarify. What's going on here?

The stark appearance of my words upon the page is in fact the *terminus ad quem* of a dynamic and at times agonizing effort of my mindbody, ensconced in my circumambient *ur*world, to enable thinking to appear in the world. Yet these verbal termini upon the page, taken by themselves, are not enough. I come back to them not from the new place that my mindbody was when its efforts culminated in the writing of the words, but instead come back to them across the landscape of this culture's dominant images, metaphors, concepts, and analogies; and it is precisely these that my thinking is undertaking to expose and impeach. My words of several weeks ago will remain opaque until I can allow my mindbody to reenter the *ur*world from out of which my thinking was accomplished in my written words. One often has this experience reading Wittgenstein. You have to come to be where Wittgenstein was, if you are to understand his cryptic words—something commonsensically expressed when we say: "I don't know where you're coming from." Often in these investigations I forget where *I'm* coming from.

8/18/87

What does it mean to claim that the whole philosophic tradition is less than truly radical? Well, of course, it is first of all to assume that through all of the chances and changes of different philosophical styles, through all the putatively opposing philosophical options, there is a motif that justifies our thinking of there *being* a "philosophic tradition." Since this tradition as we know it not only comes to us through our literacy, it may be said to be a *product* of discourse *as written*, thereby being delivered from the "evanescence, contingency, ambiguity, incoherency, and equivocation" of oral discourse (as this would be evaluated from the perspective of the putatively "stable," "coherent," and relatively unequivocal "world of literacy"), its model of reason is drawn from this world. In other words, it is *rationalistic*: its paradigm of value, meaning, and reality is the static, co-temporaneousness (in a slice of dead visual space) of the written word, easily iterable, clear, in the sense of readily available to *visual* inspection, homogeneously focal and explicit, as is each word in a succession of written words before one's gaze. It tends therefore to be biased toward claiming that that is *real*, that has *value* and *meaning*, that is *intelligible*, has a unique claim upon our attention which can be grasped and articulated in terms of this rationalistic paradigm. It tends to deny the reality of or at least to disparage all of the realities that fall beyond the range of these criteria. This of course means that the reality which incessantly and oppugnantly manifests itself in the tissues of our quotidian mind-bodily sayings and doings apart from reflection and speech, as well as that which appears and is brought into being by our casual but reflective speech, has no or an only secondary standing. In short, to be rationalistic in this sense is to draw your intellectual energy and all of your images, analogies, and metaphors for the real from the nature of the printed or written word in its sharp contrast, in many respects, with the spoken word, that is to say, to have this picture of the word at your imaginative center, radiating its formative power in all directions, like a crystal. To say this is also of course to say that the philosophical tradition is *idealistic*—not idealistic in the sense used to single out one of the perennial motifs of that tradition, but idealistic when we compare that tradition with the alternative to it that I am here advancing.

What does it mean to say that it is idealistic? It is to say—and this is, of course, a claim cognate with that having to do with its rationalism—that the philosophic tradition identifies the *real as such* with that which is exhaustively mediated in reflection through number, (written) word, and concept; therefore that *un*reality to which we have a more immediate relation, antecedent to, independent of acts of reflection—as its background and at its margins—can make but a shadowy, merely reflected appearance and can have an only equivocal standing as an object of our attention and as a value and meaning.

8/19/87

Before expanding upon this claim I must examine the phrase "... mediated in reflection through number, (written) word, and concept." As I am proposing to use the word 'idealism' to characterize the philosophic tradition as a whole in a fashion very different from its use to denominate one of the major motifs of that tradition, so I shall be using 'number', 'word', and 'concept' in a different way. It is necessary that we ask how these terms are used in the tradition.

Let us lay it down to begin with that the uses of 'word' and 'concept' will be heavily influenced by their affiliation with images of 'word' as something written and of 'concept' as having an intimate relation to 'word' as thus depicted—in short, as being cognate with 'word'. The uses of 'word' in philosophic discourse are nuanced by the paradigm of *word as printed*; and the uses of 'concept' in this same discourse cohere with the uses of 'word'.

8/24/87

What this means is that when I am engaged in reflecting critically upon the nature and status of words and concepts—as opposed to actually putting them to use in themselves—the material out of which my reflection is formed will include the ways in which my mindbody *as imagination* seizes hold of the word 'word' and the word 'concept'. If it is the disposition and culturally habituated practice of my mindbody *as imagination* to apprehend these objects as from the written or printed page—if, in other words, 'word' is essentially thought of as a *written* word, 'concept' is imagined as a "thought," a *mental* analogue of written word, derived from the *reading* of words—and, if I accept as a premise that reality is that which is mediated through word and concept *in these senses*, then the "contingent" realities (in the sense opposed to the stable and "necessary" reality of the world of writing) that appear and are known through the allegedly fugitive words and concepts that are spoken and heard in the world of orality (to say nothing of all extraverbal realities and meanings) have no serious standing *as reality*. Literacy abstracts our mindbodies *as imagination* from the dynamic flow and "transiency" (as our literate selves would have it) of the oral/aural world, endows us with marvelous new powers, but in superordinating its paradigms of reality as such, dispossesses us from our unreflected radix in the world.

[The idealism that I am imputing to the philosophic tradition is, in this sense, a creature of literacy.

[These issues can be more clearly focused if we examine the contrast between orality and literacy in more detail.]

8/25/87

The oral/aural situation typically involves at least two persons speaking and listening to one another in turn. The important events taking place in this setting—insofar as it is oral/aural—are *public*: they can be perceived by everyone. If we reconstruct this situation in our mindbodies as imagination, our habituation to this print culture will dispose us to focus almost exclusively, in our picture, upon *words*—words being spoken and words being heard, overlooking the intricate paralinguistic tapestry of meanings that inheres in the oral/aural situation—almost as if a conversation were simply the alternation of one set of disembodied verbal entities with another! And given the fact that in this literate culture 'word' has about it the aura of clarity and distinctness such as written words have appearing against the background of the surface upon which they are inscribed, we are almost certain in imagination to abstract even the *sounded* and *heard* words from the "blooming, buzzing confusion" of the oral/aural setting in which they actually appear. We imagine them to be clear and distinct even though *spoken* and *heard* because we have depicted them to ourselves as very like written and read words. In other words, we will incline to depict even the oral/aural situation as an approximation to writing and reading. Yet this is a serious misrepresentation. From the words we write and read we enjoy a certain detachment. They are over against us in a way different from the over-againstness of spoken and heard words—over against us as objects of sight are and as the objects of our hearing are not. In the oral/aural setting we are mindbodily caught up with, embrangled in, the sounds of our own and of others' voices, the convivial passions that appear, the gestures and facial expressions, the counterpoint of dialectical give-and-take, the periodization of the temporal flow which is wrought by these exchanges, thus the consequent sense of time as a dynamic passing. The speaking and hearing of words are, on this account, "events" as the writing and reading of them are not, inasmuch as they transpire in a *dynamic* "time," time that is, accordingly, different from that in which written words *endure* and the reading of them occurs— namely in the "instant." There is a sense therefore in which the reading of the written, for all of the fact that it "takes time," happens in an "eternity." Such periodization as is wrought by the comprehending glance at a succession of written or printed words is muted by comparison with that of the world of orality, because relatively abstracted by the power of sight from the immediacies of our mindbodily coition with the world. Writing and reading as we picture them are solitary activities; speaking and hearing are convivial. In our picture of orality our attention is upon speakers actually *using* the words of a language. To use a word is *to speak*, that is, quite simply to *actualize* a potentiality of our lively mindbodies in their oral/aural setting, like pointing or walking or singing a tune. It is therefore natural to say that for a speaker to "have" a concept is for him to know how to use a word; whereas printed words are not "used" in this sense, so that concepts are conceived statically—as, that is, a static mental content, like a word "printed" in the mind, or as a static form in things. It is hard to imagine a denizen of an *oral* culture picturing a concept as a static mental content which represents a statically conceived particular. If he were to be able to use the concept 'concept' at all, he would probably think of it as a word dynamically "in" a speaker's mouth, in other words, a word actually in use in a particular colloquy.

8/26/87

When I claim, then, that the philosophic tradition is an idealism, I mean that it identifies the real as such with that which is exhaustively mediated in reflection through number, word, and concept— with, that is, what is *thinkable* in word and concept, *so understood*. "Thinking" is paradigmatically—exclusively—explicit embodiment in word and concept.

8/27/87

When the imagination, imbued with the power and the values of literacy and with the authority of its images, makes this move, we come to have, not only in our formal philosophic and scientific discourse, but in the *Weltanschauung* casually but ubiquitously em-

bodied in our common sense, this "picture" of a reality that, substantial as an object of our curiosity and the recipient of our action—
in short, indubitably *real*, as we have always known it to be—is yet
not truly the bedrock of our convivial mindbodily inherence in the
world, but an abstract because reflected derivative of it.

This *thought*-world, which, even though a mark of our transcen-
dence and an instrument of our power, is not *ontologically* distinct
from or privileged vis-à-vis our "bodies"—this ideality, as I have
called it—issues in reflection from the, if you please, *ur*forms of
sensibility and the *ur*categories of the understanding that are themselves, in turn, the progeny of the sentience, orientation, motility,
and form- and meaning-discerning powers of our mindbodies.

8/28/87

However infused may be the world in which we live, move, and
have our being by the images and values of this representation of
the real, *that* world comprehends much more: all that is always and
necessarily at our backs when we are face-to-face with this "derivative" reality; all that is at the margins of our reflected pretensions;
all that is incessantly and oppugnantly asseverating itself in our
ordinary doings and sayings, our lively and tonic mindbodies as
imagination and as memory in their world.

Yet, after it has been said of the philosophic tradition that it is an
idealism in the sense developed above and is therefore less than
fully radical, since it does not disclose the actual roots of our knowing and being but rather systematically obscures them, one is led to
ask, So what? And the answer has to do mainly with its deficiencies
as philosophical anthropology.

In granting to the images of orality an only secondary authority—
images that represent us as speakers who, however incompletely
and inconstantly, own our words before one another, who make
and sometimes keep promises, as transcendent spirits, incarnate
persons—in granting these images an only secondary authority, the
philosophic tradition deprives us of these resources for doing philosophical anthropology. Such authority as they retained from our
ordinary doings and sayings throughout most of the history of that
tradition was perhaps dealt a decisive blow in the triumph of mathematics as the paradigmatic language. The rise of science and technology which resulted from this revolution further—and rapidly—
undermined the authority for us of the images of orality.

But more, the idealism of the tradition abstracted us from our pneumocarnal inherence in the world, from our mindbodily radix, thereby tempting us to angelism, precipitating us thereby into the cruel and despairing modern dialectic: man is neither an angel nor a brute. Yet—if not, then what?

11/18/87

What can we say about etymology as an ontological heuristic? How can it assist us in the discovery of the roots of being and knowing?

To begin. Etymology as I conceive it is nothing other than the attempt to disclose (by tracing the history of our language until it "disappears" into its own prehistory, that is, into the "logos" implicit in our sentience, motility, and orientation) that the world in which we dwell through our words directly and incessantly alludes to and, indeed, is dependent upon the archaic ordinations of our mindbodies; that, for example, the force and meaning of a word like 'intend' (*tendere*, to stretch) issue from and can be rendered only in terms of the very distensions of our most archaic mindbodily stretchings, that the meaning of 'abstract' (*ab*, from, and *trahere*, to draw, hence to draw away) and 'concrete' (*con*, with, and *crescere*, to grow, to wax, hence to grow together, to congeal) must cash out in the end—or rather be grounded in the beginning—as our mindbodily "drawings away" which are possible only because of our alternating "congealments" within ourselves. Of course, this line of "argument" can find no traction, if I, in reflection, systematically abscond from what is in fact *the* omnipresent reality, namely, my lively mindbody, pretending the world.

11/23/87

Etymology, then, pursued to that knot at the radix of our being into which reflection can enter hardly at all and before which intuition grows mute, discloses that *all* meaning, including, of course, the meaning-embodying, meaning-expressing powers of language, is portended in the most archaic ordinations of the mindbody's own primal energies.

Yet, how can I make such a bold and dissident claim about there being a relation between our language's history and its prehistory, on the one hand, and the usage which appears in a contemporary discourse, on the other? Indeed, is not *all* so-called usage but *use*: always necessarily *ad hoc* and occasional? This would appear to be the gravamen of the decontructionists' argument. And if all use is *ad hoc*, what connection could there possibly be between *this use* and the history and prehistory of our language. But of course, there are our "language games" and our "form of life." Does not what might be thought to be mere *use* enjoy the status of *usage* in our form of life?

[The disappointment we are almost certain to feel with the obviously, and we're inclined to say, *merely*, oral/aural authorizations of usage in "language games" and "form of life" is that of unrequited lovers of *presence*—as this is understood in Derrida's assault upon Husserl and in language-realism, which is the correlate of the doctrine of presence—who cannot, on account of our grief, recognize that the whole fabric of our oral/aural life massively and acritically rests upon them. Insofar as this is so we are subject to a heavy irony: our vision still embodies the afterimage of presence. And I'm inclined to think that here we are lethally immured in the metaphors and values of literacy—even though our oral/aural life goes on. A *real* authority, so we think, must have the permanence that the printed word has, in contrast to what we can hardly help thinking is the hopelessly fugitive existence of words spoken and heard, promises made and kept.]

11/24/87

How, then, can we render plausible the claim that contemporary feats of interpretation of what we read and hear necessarily presuppose a reliance, however tacit, however as-yet-unreflected, upon the history and even the prehistory of our language? Only by rejecting Cartesian idealism which induces us to reflect upon language (mind, thinking thing) in complete isolation from our carnal (extended thing) situation in the world—a project in which we are assisted by the values of literacy whereby language is paradigmatically *printed*, removed from the messy carnality of the actual oral/aural world.

The particular exegesis I make, usually instantaneous, of the meaning of the words I read or those I hear is a function of the texture, the form, the "grammar," the logos of "where" I am—something of which I am not explicitly aware insofar as I am focused upon the words themselves. If I wonder "where" I am before these words, I am confronted with an inexhaustible richness of answers. Attending *from* my focus upon the meaning of discourse to the "where I was" as I attended to it is precisely to change my place vis-à-vis that discourse. New questions will arise as to "where I am," I now no longer being where I was. Any answers to the question "where am I?" must be exacted from within this dialectic.

For example, when I say I am "before" the words I *read* from within a "somewhere," the force of 'before' is itself a function of that "somewhere" and likely therefore to be importantly different from that of 'before' when I say I am "before" the words I *hear*, since this will be from within a subtly, though perhaps crucially, different "somewhere" else. A good novelist places himself, his characters, and his readers in a certain "somewhere" by calling upon all the resources of his art—even though "where" he is, "where" his characters are, and "where" his readers are among themselves are not the same, nor is any of them the same throughout. The smells, the textures, the tones, colors, atmosphere, moods, and postures that constitute the ambient world of his story and that impinge upon the senses of his characters and upon the "senses" of his readers are concretely conveyed from "where" he is to "where" he would place his readers.

What are a few of the things I might say, for example, in answer to the question, "Where am I in relation to the words I read?" "What are the forms of my being in the world just now, what is the 'logic' and the 'grammar' of my situation?"

As a high school junior, aged sixteen or seventeen, living in a southern city in the midst of the Great Depression; fully sexually mature, an adolescent romantic typical of my time, aware of the other sex in an acute way; the oldest child in a family where the richness and power of the English language were at once taken for granted and celebrated; the protagonist and author of the particular story within which I see my life unfolding, a narrator who comments equivocally upon what I do as I act; the heir to a native language with its dense network of logico-etymological pretensions and retrotensions, both on its surface and in its depths, even though these are usually only known to me tacitly in my practical appreciation of the logos of this language as I practice its use—in this "where" I sat down to read Thomas Wolfe's *Look Homeward Angel*. My perceptions of the world were instantly transformed. Rereading it today at sixty-nine, in a very different "where," it seems a very different thing from the book I remember. I wonder how I could have been transported rather than put off by what I now regard as the excesses of its language.

Those elements that could be detailed as describing "where" I am, then, are as inexhaustible as the whole world of which I find myself to be a nexus.

What is of importance in all of this is the fact that *wherever* I am, it is always my historically and prehistorically dense, sentient, motile, and oriented mindbody, this ground and radix of all meaning-discernment, relying upon itself to rely upon my native language, in the texture of which the logos of its own history and prehistory asseverates itself—*wherever* I am, I say, it is always this lively, tonic ground of all meaning that is operatively implicated in my every contemporary act of interpretation.

12/1/87

And *how* does the etymology of 'intend' asseverate itself when I use it or hear it or read it?

To learn to use 'intend', 'intention', 'pretend', 'portent', 'tense', and 'tonic', is, *inter alia*, to learn to recognize the linguistic gestalt in which each will fit. In order to be able to do this we must apprehend the analogies holding among these gestalts. One of the elements which enforms these analogies, and therefore our apprehension of them in use, is their having a common etymological radical, something of which I am rarely explicitly aware, but which is implicit in the determination of the analogies. That I apprehend the uses to which these words have been put in the history of the English language and to which they can be put in the present, the roles they are capable of playing in our discourse, is in part ordained by their joint derivation from the Latin *tendere*. And if this be so, it is no exaggeration to say that the intelligence that is exhibited in my present act of formulating this argument is incarnate in the logos which enforms the sentience, motility, and orientation of my mindbody and in the history and prehistory of my language that are derivatives of them.

And what do I mean by "the prehistory of my language"? One concrete example should serve to suggest the kind of thing I mean. It has been shown that neonates *move* in precise synchrony with the articulatory structure of adult speech. These synchronous movements of infant arms and legs are elements in the prehistory of such a child's language when that is acquired. And this movement that is synchronous with speech is carried over into their skillful adult use of language in the gestural movements of their hands, the nodding of their heads in accompaniment of the rhythms of their own and others' speech.

12/2/87

The foregoing argument turns in the tightest conceivable circle. That this is so and that this is, under the circumstances, as it must be—the strictures against circularity to the contrary notwithstanding—bear closer scrutiny. The form of the argument itself embodies that situation of the thinker caught up in the world to which the *terms* of the argument would draw our attention, namely the fact, *always at the foundation of every argument*, that all meaning is rooted in the archaic ordinations of our mindbodies. All arguments in support of this claim tend to be—and appear necessarily to tend to be— but variant reiterations of the claim. There is no real *room* between the argument and its premises; between its explication and its unexplicated logico-existential ground.

First of all, in this argument, I am struck by the fact that I comprehend the meaning of 'intend' through an act of mindbodily incorporation of the word, whether it is heard or read; I *feel* the force of the word, tacitly read off the contexts of its many uses, as a kind of distension of my mindbody in its world; and I am acutely aware that without this mindbodily purchase upon the word it could mean nothing.

Then, as if to strengthen my case, I delineate the etymological affiliations of 'intend' with 'intention', 'pretend', 'portent', 'tense', and 'tonic', showing thereby that the root mindbodily feeling of tension is spread over a wider field of meaning and that, as I would claim, in each of these cases as well, I mindbodily *feel* their force as a distension.

So, this is not, and because of the nature of the case cannot be, an argument from a certain set of phenomena phenomenologically disclosed, which is then lent further support by data arrived at independently through an investigation of etymology. The etymological argument derives its whole force from the fact that it is grounded in the selfsame premise as the phenomenological one, namely, the claim that all meaning is rooted in the sentience, motility, and orientation of our mindbodies. Here I am pointing *to* the existential premise of all meaning and meaning-discernment, not arguing *from* it to a conclusion; nor am I, as if to give this premise more secure grounds, arguing from some other premise to this ground, for there are none more secure.

At this point the "argument" encroaches upon itself—as in M. C. Escher's *Drawing Hands* one hand encroaches upon and issues in the other while the other encroaches upon and gives rise to the one.

Within this narrowest ambit we come as close as language can bring us to the root and authority of all language and meaning. At such a point articulate language reveals the limits of its power fully to penetrate the concrescent reality of its users, even as it makes a reflexive reference to them; but it also discloses that the power of articulation, when acquired, remains inextricably rooted in the mind-body's orientation in the world through its prereflective exegeses of meaning, order, and value; and, finally, it shows that our speech and writing, be their vectors ever so abstract, can never be wholly alienated from the logos of these primitive ordinations.

None of our languages—"ordinary language," the language of pure mathematics, the language of poetry, the languages of fable and myth, each of course obeying its own grammar, but for present purposes all of a piece—are ever disaffiliated from the world that, by their very utterance, is brought forth from that world's hitherto unarticulated ground. In short, an ecumenic claim that these languages *must* fail of their telos is, on its face, absurd.

12/7/87

I need to explore the very complicated relation between what we *do* and what we *say* about what we do, and how what we say about what we do plays into what we do. Even this framing of the problem is a gross oversimplification. All the nonsense which has been uttered on what has been taken to be the neat and unambiguous distinction between theory and practice—with the derivative argument against theory—needs to be challenged. And of course a part of what requires attention here is the role played by what I have analyzed elsewhere as the picture which we at once *have* and are *in the midst of* and the notion of our *theater of reflection* in our *acts* of reflection. What needs examination, in short, is my *mindbody as imagination*.

12/10/87

By reason of the logos which enforms our sentience, motility, and orientation we have a world. These powers of ours are *powers* precisely insofar as they embody and express this formal order. Our most elementary forms of sensory experience are disposed toward their telos by the operative intentionalities of our several senses, these rooted in their turn in the formal causes of biotic life. Our ordered motility and orientation that form our world and that direct us to that world as it is formed consolidate as a final cause the formal causes upon which they depend. The efficacy of this operative logos is not dependent upon its being reflected. What is of importance here is that it is this as-yet-unreflected logos that issues in our reflected life, which never ceases to depend upon the former and with which it therefore is continuous. This continuity between the as-yet-unreflected and reflection—between, to use Husserl's distinction, operative intentionality and active intentionality—is the setting in which an investigation of the relation between what we do and what we say about what we do—between, that is, practice and theory—must be conducted.

12/11/87

If what I have said above is indeed the case, then there is no human activity which is not enformed by a logos, a telos, a meaning. An attack of *grande mal* may be, humanly speaking, a mere "brute event." But few—very few—of our activities can be said to be. It is irrelevant that we carry out large classes of these activities without comment, without any second-order description and appraisal, without any explicit recognition of the logos that enforms them. Their "rationality," their subordination to a larger framework of order and meaning, does not depend upon their being reflected as such. But then this is self-evident. Why have I found it to be remarkable?

The answer lies, I think, in the direction from which I came upon this discovery: from the question about the relation between practice and theory. When I pose this question the Cartesian dualism is there for me to fall into; to be tempted to think that practice (abstractly considered) is ontologically distinct from theory and discontinuous with it as, subject to the Cartesian picture that we both *have* and are *in the midst of*, the as-yet-unreflected is discontinuous with reflection and my brutish body is with my mind.

If we now talk about this question in the light of the above, we shall see that the important distinction for us is that between practice (what I do, what I am given to doing) upon which I have *not* explicitly reflected and am *not now* reflecting, and practice which *has* been the subject of reflection and appraisal.

12/14/87

The relation between practice and theory thus comes to be seen as extraordinarily complex—far more complex than the rather crude accounts, ignorant of concrete cases, would have it. Yet—these crude accounts—even they stand to our practice *as theory is alleged to stand to practice according to these accounts.* If the accounts are, as I claim, defective, then how have they failed to impede our practice? In other words, what jobs do these accounts *do*, after all, if even defective ones fail to impede practice? Do more adequate ones facilitate it? And what, by the way, does 'adequate' mean here? Defective accounts do not impede practice because these accounts, insofar as they enter into practice at all, are tacitly corrected by the logos already inherent in practice.

Part of the problem lies in the fact that we overlook "intermediate cases"—as Wittgenstein says. The words 'theory' and 'practice' are used in different contexts and in differing relations to one another in a multitude of ways.

Let us take Freud as a case. In his clinic, actually engaged in transactions with a patient, he is saying and doing what he says and does in response to the contingent sayings and doings of the patient. If asked by the critic in his head, "What's going on here," he replies, "A psychoanalysis," thereby introducing a whole theoretical framework through which to observe—as a participant observer—*what* he is doing while he is in the process of doing it. Doing what he is doing and observing and appraising what he is doing go on side by side in a dialectical exchange.

Freud's brilliant case studies are narratives derived from his exchanges with his patients having a larger, more comprehensive view of what is going on than is possible in these day-to-day exchanges. The more comprehensive telos—"an analysis"—is presupposed. The relation between this emerging narrative account and the recollection of the content of the day-to-day exchanges is similarly dialectical. And in the background there stands the model of the human psyche developed in the "Project of 1895."

12/15/87

But there is, of course, more. There is the ethos of early 20th-century medical practice and research, dominated, in Freud's case, by the aspiration to and expectation of an exhaustively physiological topography of the human being, which Helmholtz had articulated. This in turn was translated into the style and the values of clinical practice. Who and what I am as a doctor in relation to who and what you are as a patient is established by this style and by these values.

Clearly the case studies, the "Project of 1895," and the style and values of clinical practice conveyed to the young Freud in his apprenticeship do not all bear the same logical relationship to his developing practice, whatever this now greatly complexified concept may be said to mean; yet it would be difficult to claim that they do not *all* bear upon it.

The judgments of the critic in Freud's head, the articulations of who the patient is, provided in the case studies, the "Project of 1895," and the style and values embodied in clinical practice *all*—more or less explicitly, more or less directly or obliquely—provide the theater within which Freud carries on his practice. What Freud does and what he *chooses* to do are defined by this framework of concepts and images. They provide the form and telos of his activity. And then there is, of course, Freud's classical education in the *Gymnasium* and Goethe's dissenting views on nature which he read and admired.

Obviously these motifs are not all logically equidistant from actual practice. Furthermore, thinking about the *particulars* of the "Project of 1895" with a view to constructing a model as a thing in itself, on one hand, and thinking about them, or more exactly thinking through them, by means of them—once the model has been achieved—on the other, are logically heterogeneous activities. They each may however be said to "say" something to Freud as to what he is doing, to afford him options for understanding and authorizing what he might do.

What begins to emerge in these reflections is the fact that the concepts and images which form the logos and telos of practice are heterogeneous in relation to each other and that most of them function at a tacit level most of the time. Further, even the way in which highly reflected theories and models bear upon our practice cannot be simply stated, since, for one thing, their bearing is subject to the dialectical exchanges between their explicit and tacit forms; and because these dynamically interact with the whole repertoire of other explicit and tacit concepts and images that define the situation. And this whole process of dialectical exchange among these images and values and among the several levels that appear in our analysis is subject to the integration—both tacit and explicit—deriving from the center of Freud's being as engaged in practice.

One consequence of these disclosures would appear to be this: such connection as there might be between explicit *accounts* of the processes of thinking and our *actual* thinking is something that is *tacitly* supplied, and therefore likely to be systematically overlooked in any *explicit* account. This is a complicated way of saying that the actual *roots* of reflection are ultimately beyond the reach of explicitation.

It may also be observed that Freud in his metapsychological writing chose to use idiomatic German instead of the coinages deriving from Greek, adopted by Strachey and other translators into English in the attempt to make his writings more "scientific."* His straightforward, commonsensical German, as he uses it, imparts to him, in the very language itself, a certain sense of what it is he is doing rather than some other.

12/18/87

A good deal seems to be made among deconstructionists of their claim that our linguistic usage is a (mere) convention. This assumption of the relativity of our language to time and place issues on occasion in a kind of dynamic nihilism which seems to energize the movement.

Yet, what does this claim amount to? In one sense, it is easy enough to say: linguistic usage is subject to time and place. A bland and hardly controversial claim—as a look at the *O.E.D.*, organized "on historical principles," will disclose.

12/21/87

For the deconstructionists and their followers this seems an *exciting* discovery. We need to ask how it is they come upon this truism in such a way as to find it to be heavy with philosophic import.

Two distinctions need to be made. First, that between my *use*—

[* Bruno Bettelheim.]

my asseveration—of words in any and every linguistic situation whatsoever, on the one hand, and, on the other, the *style* in which I dwell in these asseverations. Second, the distinction between speaking and reading aloud. They are not the same.

If I, in good faith, make a solemn promise, I do not (must not) equivocate at all. By contrast, equivocation is the very soul of irony. When playing Hamlet on the stage my relation to the words of Shakespeare is, on the equivocation scale, somewhere betwixt and between. In all these speech-acts words are *used* to serve three different sorts of ends and accordingly exhibit differing degrees or forms of equivocation. In none however is there any equivocation affecting the *authority of the words in use as vectors of meaning*. Whatever the style I adopt, in the act of speaking, my words are acritically authoritative *as words in use*.

Because the words of my native language have *de facto* had absolute authority over me as the very condition of my acquiring it in the course of the history of this acquisition, within the mindbodily convivium of my fellow native speakers, they have now come to have *de jure* authority. [To be quite exact, my words exert their authority over me at a logical and ontological level antecedent to the existence of the *de facto/de jure* distinction.] Therefore we instantly recognize the words and their uses—which is to say, they have long since served us as vectors of meaning both *before* the question of meaning has been raised and *after* our reflected skepticism has allegedly impeached their "authority" as nothing more than "conventional." No second-order theory or vindication of the authority of our language—including an appeal to the authority of conventional usage—could remotely approach the weight of that which is rooted in our actual unequivocal and confident convivial *use* of our words, for here there is no room to insert even the sharp knife-edge of skepticism. Indeed, this primordial authorization is not only the *ground* of the concept of authority, itself grounded in our mindbodily being in the world; it is the touchstone for our use of the concept.

To say that our linguistic usage is a convention—if it is to be understood as more than the tautology that linguistic usage is linguistic usage, i.e., that certain patterns of practice can be observed in our speech-community—is to claim, it would appear, that these practices have a certain *authority*—an authority deriving from the fact of a "coming together," an agreement. Our usage is thought to be *authorized* by this agreement: authority is *conferred* by consent, even if only tacit.

Yet, what does this mean? It could not possibly mean that our native language was *constituted* in convention, albeit this picture of a social compact among rational agents is deeply entrenched in our Enlightenment imaginations and serves to reinforce our belief that our usage is not (merely) a brute social fact (whatever this might be), but commands authority over us.

If no such explicit "coming together" can be imagined; and if, nevertheless, the social fact of usage is conceived to have authority, then its authority must be grounded elsewhere than in a compact among consenting adults. And the question then becomes, Where? Is it possible that this "authorization" derives from *tacit* forms of coming together, unreflected modes of affiliation and acculturation which are antecedent to our *explicit*, reflected, and more or less lucid acts of assent and that command especial weight, not *in spite of, but because of* this fact. Could it be that the myth of a social compact is the device by which the Enlightenment retains, all un-witting to be sure, the authority that it would explicitly deny but here tacitly recognizes as inherent in our earliest forms of "coming together," our primordial, unreflected modes of affiliation—in our nursing at the maternal breast, in our entry into the suburbs of our native language as we follow with our infant gestures the lilt of our mothers' speech?

It is not however that in calling our usage a convention we mean no more than to claim that a so-called "brute social fact" has author-ity over us—whether this claim is advanced in terms of the model of a social compact or, alternatively, in terms of an appeal to our pri-mordial feats of affiliation as neonates. There is a negative import in this claim: the claim, namely, that our usage is a *mere*, a *nothing more than*, convention. And we need to ask: " 'mere' compared to what"? What would be a better basis, if we did but have it, for the authority of our usage than this "mere"? The answer is, as I have suggested elsewhere, language realism.

What is the relationship that we imagine ourselves as having to our words such that we are led to entertain the skeptical view that our language is a "mere convention"?

12/22/87

How am I represented as perceiving, knowing, existing in time, judging and acting according to the imaginative structures, images, metaphors, values, pictures, and motifs that are always at my back?

Am I depicted here as a spectator who beholds static objects distanced from me by sight in a slice of dead visual space? Is the time in which I exist paradigmatically the static time of the mere endurance of physical objects? Are my feats of judgment seen to be the lucid acts of an essentially contextless arbiter confronted by explicit options? And is my action the exercise of the power to do or not do a given thing? If so, then the imaginative forms at my back are dominated by the values and motifs that derive in reflection from the activity of reading printed texts—my relation to this object distanced by the sense of sight, as I imagine, as no "object" of our aural sense could ever be; distanced and therefore always detached, no matter how absorbed I may become. I can "hold at arm's length" what I read, can thus get a "firm grip" upon it and, therefore, given this value of literacy par excellence, regard it as having peculiar authority, by the mere fact of its standing on the printed page.

If, on the other hand, the values of my residual oral/aural life prevail, then the metaphors in which I represent knowing and perceiving to myself will be drawn from the intimacies of my oral/aural exchanges; where the distancing of their "objects" does not occur (in that sense of 'distancing' appropriate to a description of the world of sight and seeing); where the context of feats of judging is rich, complex, and at times intrusive; where the temporal setting of my existence is taken to be primarily the forward surge of oral/aural time, periodized by its dialectical exchanges.

My conception of what words are and how I am related to them in speaking and in reading, my conception of the vectors of meaning and how it is borne by them, my view as to what is stable and what fugitive—how and why—will be different according to whether my imagination is subject to the values of literacy or to those of my residual orality.

Even though the values of alphabetic literacy have been superordinate in Western culture since the invention of printing and the propagation of the printed book, we remain residually oral/aural. It therefore should not surprise us, if we find the values, images, metaphors, and paradigms of both modes of the appearance of the word and both ways of interpreting these modes conflated in our imaginations.

12/23/87

When I think about my relation to the words I *speak* under the suasion of metaphors and paradigms drawn from my oral/aural experience, what is spoken and what is heard retaining, as they do, an intimate connection with my mindbodily center, the relation strikes me as at once *necessary*—it is the *conditio sine qua non* of the existence as such of spoken words—and *incommutable*—I cannot, according to this depiction, speak the words I am just now speaking and, *at the same time*, speak just any words whatsoever.

When my thought about my relation to the words I read is governed by the images and values implicated in the practice of reading texts, as this is conceived in our literate visualist culture, wherein the printed words are alienated from my center by vision, the distancing sense, the relation strikes me as at once *contingent*—the words are not bound to me by a dependency for their existence upon my reading of them—and *commutable*—the visible words on the page, no matter how absorbing they may be, are abstract, stripped of the concrete resonances of the oral/aural setting, and thus having but an equivocal and tenuous bond to me in my concrete actuality.

And if, in imagination, I abstract myself one step further in order to formulate a theory of the status of texts, of words on a page, of words spoken and of meaning, the words now under consideration are likely to have become, in my reflection, no longer particular words, but any printed words whatsoever, and therefore *infinitely* commutable. Thus is well begun the process of the radical destabilization of meaning, in no way even suggested, even less implied, by the nature of the actual oral/aural exchanges of our quotidian life, where the efficacy of our acts of speech and their vectors is never subject to *radical* doubt nor felt to be contingent and commutable in any sense.

In this theater of reflection it is very likely that speaking will be imagined to be a *reading aloud*. I will begin to think that my relation to the words I *speak* is as contingent and fungible as my relation to the words I *read*. At the same time, the permanence and stability of printed words (as compared to that of the words in the *actual* oral/aural reciprocity) is eroded. It's as if printed words, while remaining "visible," are torn from the surface of the page, thereby surrendering their permanence as fixed objects in visual space, yet retaining their contingency in their relation to a reader. Their existence is thus imagined to be more transitory than the concrete resonances of remembered words in the actual fabric of oral/aural life; and their relation to me, their speaker, who, in this picture, *reads them aloud*, is represented as being as contingent and commutable as the relation to me of the printed words I read. "Spoken" words, that is, words now imagined as being read aloud, are, as vectors of meaning, according to this imaginative representation, both fugitive and fortuitous; no less so is the meaning that they bear.

Though "spoken" words are fugitive and contingent, they also lose, when depicted as *read aloud*, that real, essentially different sense of the radical non-necessitation of the uttered and personally owned words that issue from my mouth as I speak. In short, they lose their true character *as oral*. Thus the values of our residual orality are muted or entirely obscured: suppressed as a resource for the overcoming of the nihilism that seems easily to issue from this theater of reflection.

The equation "Speaking is reading aloud" not only falsifies the nature of speech. By introducing into our conception of our relation to texts the dynamism and indeterminacy of the oral/aural reciprocity, subject to the forward surge of time, it also misrepresents the nature of texts and reading.

12/25/87

Derrida's doctrine of *differance* could not sustain the interest or generate the pathos it has but for these facts. Viewed from the perspective of the static values of printed words in visual space, it is a truism, bearing with it no pathos on its own. It comes to the following: a word could not be the bearer of a meaning if it were used by only one person on only one occasion (what could it possibly mean to speak of a 'word' under these conditions?). If, then, it is to serve as a vehicle of meaning, it must be *iterable*, i.e., usable on many different occasions by many different speakers in many different contexts. Yet the extent to which it satisfies this requirement, i.e., is iterable, is precisely the extent to which the meaning of a sign cannot be exhaustively *present* to itself—if, that is, to be "present" is to be "in sight" and to be "out of sight is to be out of mind." In any given instance a word has at once to mean what it does in *this* context and also *not* mean all the things it does in *other* contexts. To cast this home truth in the sort of paradoxical language that so amuses the Derridians: a word means what it does not mean and does not mean what it means. Construed in a certain way, true enough. This is *differance*!

The scandal here is that no one in real life imagines that this truism has the import imputed to it by the deconstructionists; and this fact is not philosophically trivial. Thus do words come to be thought of as *mere* conventions; thus is accomplished the abolition of man.

And why is it that a certain excitement accompanies the deconstructionist "discovery" of this fact? It is because modernity is addicted to the drug of dynamic nihilism, which requires larger and larger doses and grows more and more immune to the criticism which would be the beginning of a cure.

12/29/87

We can no more in good faith regard our form of life, insofar as we dwell in it, as a mere brute "social" fact than we can regard our bodies, insofar as they are ours, as mere brute "physical" ones. These cannot be brute facts precisely because the *ur*meanings that issue in *all* structures of order and value are embodied in the very warp and woof of their existence as such, logically/ontologically antecedent to the distinction between fact and value.

The objectivity from within which we come to take as mere facts certain elements of the one and certain parts of the other can itself be sustained only by our form of life and our bodies. They stand to this detached view of things as tradition stands to critical thought.

Yet this is a far too abstract way of depicting our relation to tradition. We are inclined in the context of Enlightenment to view it too rationalistically. In our rationalism we are likely, in making a claim about tradition and criticism such as the above, to picture the relation between the former and the latter as like that between premises and conclusions, wherein the first and the second and their relation to one another lie open to our intellectual inspection in the same ahistorical instant, suggesting that we are "outside" tradition and thus can have a lucid prospect upon it. All the elements of their relations, according to this picture, are taken to be logically homogeneous, suggesting that tradition and criticism have the same logical standing and, more important, that they have the same *kind* of weight; that tradition exerts its force in the way that an explicitly reflected premise does when construed in the light of the above rationalistic model, whereas the force of all the *unreflected* premises, metaphors, analogies, images, pictures which determine the range and limits—*and power*—of critical thought is hardly *felt* at all—in that way of being felt associated with the "context" of an act of conscious reflection with an item of explicit knowledge. Yet its potency, far from being less on this account, is in fact more. Indeed, in the case of a neurotic construction of reality, the power over us of the picture is enhanced by its unavailability to ordinary conscious awareness and is accessible at all only after protracted psychotherapy.

If tradition as that which is handed over, *given*—whether as one's native language, a practice, inherited analogies, metaphors, imaginative pictures—exerts its force in such a way as hardly to be felt by us, though not less potent on this account, it is that within which we dwell at ease. It is that upon which we most intimately depend, that upon which we, our "wakefulness," our care, our effort, our skepticism suspended, can rely; it is our home. We are *at home* in the world insofar as we dwell in our lively mindbodies in the matrices of our form of life. To suffer from bad conscience because of this—as is the Enlightenment's way—to, alternatively, talk in Heideggerian terms of our being "thrown" into the world does not alter the *fact* of our having been "handed over" to ourselves precisely by that which has formed and continues to sustain us. It serves only to fashion an *Enlightenment* myth in the light of which we are declared to be homeless. And so we have taken ourselves to be since Descartes handed us our deracinate *cogito*.

1/20/88

The ironies in our discourse around which, it may be supposed, important business with "imaginary/real" is conducted are exemplified by the following quite ordinary case.

You say to me, "I am going to Atlantis." I reply, "How?" You answer, "By TWA." For an instant puzzled, I ask, "Is this Tinkerbell World Airways, Third World Airways, or Trans World?" Even in so uncomplicated a case, so ordinary, indeed, that we cannot imagine being puzzled by it, there is a great deal of play, among implied senses of 'imaginary' and 'real'. Is Atlantis real—e.g., the Aegean island of Thera—or is it imaginary—a place in the heart. If it is the former, we will require Trans World Airways. If the latter, Tinkerbell will do. But perhaps Auden's poem "Atlantis" is the best vehicle of all by which to be borne to the Atlantis of the heart.

In sorting out this situation it seems natural and harmless to distinguish between an Aegean island and an island in the heart, using the distinction imaginary/real. From this we cannot conclude however that one or the other of these has in some ultimate, context-neutral sense a better standing; for all of the pretensions of our mindbodies to the places in their world—whether islands in the

Aegean or islands in the heart—bear equally upon *places*, with equal "reality" in the fabric of the world which is that actively cohering system of meaning at the center of which we at every moment find ourselves.

1/21/88

I find myself just now *remembering* the events of yesterday; *recalling* fragments of a dream I was having as I awoke this morning; *attending* to the words emerging from the tip of my pen, *checking* for their legibility; *hearing* the washing machine chugging away in the background; *struggling* to formulate these reflections while avoiding the pitfalls of the philosophically traditional ways of formulating them; *recalling* a conversation with Pat as she was leaving in which she reminded me of several chores I need to do; in fragments, *fantasizing* doing them: seeing the drive-up window at the cleaners, the man who serves at this window; seeing myself cashing a check at the bank machine, *picturing* myself—yes it will be the Mercedes 280 SL—*driving* toward Chapel Hill on Old Chapel Hill road; *thinking* "tomorrow is Friday, lunch with the Raj Quartet"; etc., etc. If I abscond from my locus at the plexus of these activities in order to contemplate them in a detached manner, they and, what will at this very moment become for the first time, their "objects" will undergo a fundamental change. Their *de facto* integration in the fabric of my unreflecting mindbody will dissolve; and these several activities will become *objects* for reflection, standing over against me.

1/26/88

At one moment I am simply moving within the very pith of my ordinary doings—with, to be sure, a sidelong glance in order to notice their texture; in the very next I have by means of this print culture's theater of reflection, with its esteem for the visible and for stasis, abstracted myself from my ordinary doings, in order, it is assumed, to reflect upon their *true* nature. What I discern of course is their "true nature" as they appear *in this theater of reflection*—not as actual, lively doings unfolding in time to my sidelong glance, but as static reflection-objects.

Until this shift all these pretensions, and of course many others I have not singled out, cohere seamlessly in the natural bonds provided by my lively, ductile mindbody—each of these pretensions, throughout this moment, enjoying equal "ontological" weight, all together composing the world in which I find myself during the passage of time roughly represented by the above catalog of activities.

Is this solipsism? Is reality composed of a mere multiplicity of momentary worlds—windowless monads with no communication among them? Not at all. The world is exactly as we have always known it to be: ". . . Out there as a mountain's poise of stone, the world is present, about, and I know that I am, here, not alone, but with a world . . ." (W. H. Auden). Rather, my world, *our* world—whether through the dreams we share or our common perceptions of the physical world; whether within this very moment or within such a span of time as includes those now long dead and those as yet unborn—is far richer than the world that appears, and in appearing is immediately privileged, in our critical reflection. Yet this richer world is the primitive one in which we *never cease* to live and move and have our being.

What is it in the nature of this shift to critical reflection that obscures and tacitly denigrates this primitive world? The answer lies, I think, in the shift from orality to literacy—the substitution of written words for their lively speaking as the preeminent metaphor for the real. Printing elevates the realm of the visible even more decisively to a new status and a new value. This propagation of alphabetic literacy was of course coeval with the beginning of the Enlightenment which Greek philosophy was.

As a result of this great transformation the *real*, the *truly* existent, comes to be thought to be whatever perdures in (visual) space and time *in the way that printed (or written) words perdure* in (visual) space and in the time which is the coordinate of this space.

Thus is the concept of "a (public) space of appearance" preempted for use in this new order of things. The "space of appearance" comes to mean exclusively the (visual) space within which visible objects appear and among which we can move about freely, inspecting them, if we wish, from all sides—either actually or virtually. Our ordinary linguistic usage is richer and more faithful. We are, in this new order, given to supposing quite uncritically that an 'object' is an extended entity perduring in visual space and that we can find *in our path*, over against our bodies as the chair over which we stumble is against them. The "objection" to your argument is no such three-dimensional impediment in (visual) space, yet it is experienced by you as something *over against you* in an absolutely primordial, underived, and intractable sense, for all that it is but words floating toward you on the air.

The paradigm of the real comes to be precisely what can appear here. What can appear here only equivocally or not at all is no part of or no *real* part of the real world.

Written words are visible, spoken words are not; written words are static, spoken words are dynamic; written words are over against me as objects in (visual) space, spoken words are not over against me *in this way*; with written words I retain a large degree of detachment—one might say a kind of distance and autonomy—with spoken words, especially when addressed to me personally, I am globally caught up. This opposition between my body in (visual) space and the static, perduring written or printed word before me is the source of our conception of objectivity in the West. We can only barely guess how profoundly our sensibility of Enlightenment has shaped our second-order account of things—even though, for all of this, we have never ceased to live in the primitive world from which reflection derives and upon which it never ceases to depend.

The world in which I find myself when I am at the very heart of my ordinary doings, where the putatively *real* car I drive seamlessly coheres with the *fantasy* conversation I simultaneously conduct—with no distinction between them *in that world* as to their legitimate standing *as elements of that world*—the value and authority of this world cannot survive the shift in our sensibility wrought by literacy. And yet we never cease to live in it. This is why the myths in the midst of which I live my life are no more just engrafted onto my *real* life than is my fantasy conversation merely extrinsic to my activity of driving my car. All of these modes of my mindbody's being are integrated and sustained in my intentional mindbody. Had what I think of as the privileged realm of physical reality no other and better integration with myth and fantasy than that *extrinsically* achieved by critical reflection, I should collapse in a heap. The achievement of a coherent logos among the many modalities in which I dwell in the world—a coherence among which that is at times so problematic for reflection that I resort to reducing all or some of these modes to a few others of them—is the work of my lively mindbody uninhibited by, because not requiring, any abstraction from its own intentional integrity. This is the archaic coherence upon which I unreflectingly rely for the living of my life. It is also this from which the reflected distinction between "reality" and "myth" derives.

When I am *actually* engaged in speaking or driving a car no distinction appears to my sidelong glance between these activities and something placed over against them. My speaking when it is actually being done has no object—no L. *ob* + *iectum*, no Ger. *Gegenstand*. Nor does my activity of driving a car. To my driving *as activity* there is no car over against me; nor even any road *over-against it*.

2/2/88

The world-forming power, the "reality"-bearing authority of the realms of myth, ritual, and fantasy—to mention only these—are at a single stroke impeached in the transformation of our sensibility through the propagation of alphabetic literacy.

And yet the temporal distentions of my lively mindbody within which a day, a decade, a lifetime have their worldly subsistence and reality are the selfsame distentions that are the setting and vectors of even my most narrowly defined sense perceptions; and that are indeed the *conditio sine qua non* of their appearing.

When I read this over, that philosophically still-unreconstructed part of myself says: "Idealism!" Is this idealism? No, it is not. But why do I impulsively suspect idealism?

2/4/88

Is it not because when I, as in this instance, contemplate the world I have been describing, I have, by virtue of reflection, absconded from the heart of my own ordinary doings. When I do this, of course, I unwittingly embrace the philosophic tradition's paradigm of the real: that which like the written and printed word is constant, static, and perduring in (visual) space. *From this perspective* the world of my description appears unstable, fugitive, and, above all, as free-floating as human consciousness, without anchorage in anything more constant than its elements? It is this quality of this *described* world that provokes the panicky thought: "Idealism!"

But of course the world I have described above is one into which the distinction between real–less real–unreal has not and cannot enter; even less the application of the printed word in (visual) space as paradigm of the real. By the time it does we are ontologically elsewhere. Where we shall be will be a function of our theater of reflection. As we've discovered, for us this is usually one formed by alphabetic literacy. The truth is, my dreams and fantasies, be they ever so fugitive, are as firmly grounded in my lively mindbody as are my sense perceptions of the physical world. Like them, they are the pretensions of my mindbody; no less than they, they retrotend it: the substantial, unremitting, and omnipresent attestation of reality—though neither as substantial nor as unremitting as the static printed word in (visual) space is taken to be—and the ground of meaning, meaning-discernment, order, and value.

My fantasies, your fantasies—our mutual fantasies, if we choose to share them, as we regularly do—have, then, as good grounds as our sense perceptions of the physical world, because they have the *same* grounds. Yet this does not at all mean that we cannot discriminate between sense perceptions and fantasies in the service of any of a number of different purposes. It is only to assert that they have equal standing as possible elements in our world at any given moment; that neither is *in principle* privileged in some context-neutral way, but rather is privileged in the context of some particular interest—epistemological or practical—that we might have as over against some other interest.

For example, if we thought that a large part of our lives had as its setting a communal dream of a sacred time given form by myths about gods and humankind, their "enactment" attended by rituals, we probably would make quite acute tacit distinctions between the affairs of "profane life"—without necessarily identifying them as such—and those of "sacred time" when these were in practice called for—however, without an election between their respective ontological weights, and without assuming that these orders do not continually interpenetrate in the fabric of our actual living.

I have said that this world—my world, our world at any given moment—consists in the pretensions of my mindbody, our convivial mindbodies. It needs to be reiterated that the mindbody's substantiality and constancy are *conveyed* in its pretensions and retrotensions—what it pretends and what retrotends it. Or to be more exact, within any given temporal distention, that which is the form of my mindbodily existence *is* its pretensions and retrotensions.

One of the great ironies of the contemporary academic scene: people are the oppressed captives of the ideology of "ideology." It relieves everyone of the burden of thought. I wish I could laugh! The ideological explanation of "thought"—which within limits is very illuminating—produces its special form of intellectual complacency. In arguing that the decisive determination of thought is achieved in its material conditions, reductive ideological explanations displace the thinker—who, for it, really cannot exist. We are thereby subtly relieved of responsibility for what we think and say. On its face, it is somehow more plausible than a behavioristic reductionism. Subtle and insidious.

2/17/88

In detailing some of the motifs that enform the practice of Freud— called "motifs" because they appear in his practice as recurring figures and therefore impart to it a certain form; but also because it is these that *move* (as in *motive*) him toward a certain telos—I have mentioned his daily transactions with his patients in the idiom of their mutual native language; the emerging metapsychology which served to identify the meaning of the phrase "a psychoanalysis"; the narrative accounts of his patients' histories, drawn from his daily exchanges with them; the model of the psyche developed in the "Project of 1895"; the style and values of 20th-century medical practice, introjected by Freud in his apprenticeship; the classical education he received in the *Gymnasium*; his reading in Goethe's philosophy of nature—to single out only these. All of these, and of course many others, compose the rich texture of Freud's imagination and give meaning and form to what he does, what he is given to doing. And I have suggested that there is rather complex play among these, sometimes explicit, perhaps usually tacit; alternately unreflected and reflected; all motifs enjoying the same weight in all of these modes, all having essentially the same potency. And then I say, "Obviously these motifs are not all logically equidistant from actual practice," and I wonder what this can mean?

To say "Not all of these motifs are equidistant from (an) actual practice" is to say that some are more inclusive in their range than others. *Some* of the motifs of *my* practice, after all, enter into everything I do. The difference between one thing I do and another is the difference between the repertoire of other motifs, with an increasingly narrow range of logical efficacy, that enter into the one and into the other. When however I am engaged in any given practice, every motif that enforms the doing and that, together, determines it as *this* doing rather than *that* one carries equal weight. Taken together they constitute the logos of my practice. By the same token we may speak of the logos that enforms the convivial practice of a people.

What is the purpose of this analysis which, once written out, seems self-evident? To show that the relation between what we do and what we say about what we do is far more complex than is suggested by the rather glib current discussions of theory and practice, since the very idea of a practice is far richer than these suggest. Can the ideas of a theory be less so?

It is worth observing that these several motifs could not be made to cohere by some incredible act of explicit plotting of their abstract logical connections, since, strictly, none exist. For example there is no way to bring the rich conception of a patient, such as Freud had while in the midst of a lively exchange with her, into logical accord with the topography of the psyche that is set forth in "The Project of 1895." These two views are *logically* incommensurable. We conceive them as otherwise only because we tacitly provide, usually unwittingly of course, a *tertium quid*, namely, an actual context—the practitioner—who views the patient first in one way and then in the other—and therefore, *in a real sense*, simultaneously from within both at once—and in whose *practice* those are made to cohere that could not be made to do so in theory, that is, from a detached standpoint.

2/23/88

It begins to appear that in the light of the positions set forth in *Polanyian Meditations* both theory and practice—however useful and, indeed, necessary the distinction between them may be in particular contexts—are ultimately grounded in the mindbody's sentience, motility, and orientation. For beings like ourselves whose "practices" and "theories" derive their telos and their form, with equal radicality, from the logos implicated in our mindbodies, there can be no ultimately practice-free theory, no essentially theory-neutral practice. It is therefore impossible to argue to an absolute, context-neutral distinction between theory and practice, since both of these *always* refer back to their ground in which the distinction becomes blurred and then disappears. The *form* of the movements of the muscles of my body in a given activity and the *ordinations* of my body that *give* them that form are one and the same. In short, there is no theory that is not connate with, as consequent is with antecedent, the most archaic ordinations of our mindbodies' primordial energies.

Now, of course, I am sentient, motile, and oriented because I do not exist in the instant; because, in other words, my mindbody is temporal and intentional; distended between no-longer and not-

yet. This is a truism whose ontological and epistemological significance must not be overlooked. The various forms that at various
times mediate this pretensive/retrotensive structure of my being
are *motifs*—as I called them above, in discussing Freud's practice—
but that can quite as profitably be called *theories*.

Theory here refers to a certain "view" or a mode of "viewing" or
a means of "viewing"—a painting by Masaccio or Cézanne provides
me with views of the space of vision, though very different ones,
and they are therefore, in my sense, *theories*; but equally J. S. Bach's
A Musical Offering and Schoenberg's *Moses und Aron* may be said to
provide me with two different "views" and two different modes of
"viewing" time, and are therefore equally, in my sense, *theories*—
theory here refers to a device that serves to induce a certain disclosure, that performs a heuristic function, that holds and directs
attention, that gives a particular structure to that temporal opening
at the heart of my being between no-longer and not-yet and in
doing this broadens the scope and complexity of my vista within
time. Elsewhere I have interpreted metaphor so as to be able to see it
as theory. It would be more accurate to say that the painting case
and the music case present me with different ways of *being* in space
and time; and that if I behold Cézanne as I listen to Schoenberg, I
shall dwell in space-time in a different way from that in which I
dwell if I behold Masaccio as I listen to Bach.

When Odysseus washes ashore after shipwreck, covered with
brine and his own blood, he is found by Nausicaa, the daughter of
the King of the Phaeacians. After being bathed and adorned with
rich garments he becomes the honored guest at a banquet of the
royal court. When the feasting is over, Nausicaa accompanies herself
on her lyre as she sings the story of one Odysseus, his deeds and his
sufferings. Upon hearing his own story, set before him as a thing in
the public space of the banquet, Odysseus *sees* his life for the first
time and, as Hannah Arendt comments, "sheds the tears of remembrance." The narrative is a kind of *timescape* for action and passion
within which Odysseus can see his life. So regarded, Nausicaa's
song is a *theory*. Surely Isak Dinesen expresses a similar view when
she says: "All sorrows can be borne, if we put them into a story."
When the scope of our vista within time is broadened in this way we
no longer remain merely passive to our suffering.

Let us imagine that Freud, because he had read *Oedipus Tyrannus*
in *Gymnasium*, was able suddenly to see certain data from his colloquies with patients, heretofore meaningless in themselves, as the
particulars of a temporal configuration that was to become known

as an Oedipus Complex. Put into the story of Oedipus these previously unconnected data became elements of an intelligible whole. Accomplishing this the story functions as a heuristic device, a *theory* serving to disclose.

The efficacy of our motility and orientation is effected not alone by the broadening of our scope by means of a theory; it is effected as well by its systematic contraction, as with a map. A map of North Carolina which was exactly the size of the state would be useless.* A projection drawn to a manageable scale not only orients us when a state-sized map could not; it is possessed of heuristic power because on it we can show the distribution of population in relation to elevation and the course of rivers. Theories not only expand our knowledge by expanding our scope. They expand it by means of a systematic and rational contraction of it. A map is a *theory* of this latter sort.

2/24/88

Our language, too, is a *theory* of great heuristic power. Like a map in certain respects, it achieves this by a systematic contraction of and abstraction from the as-yet-unreflected structure of prelingual experience. A language possessing no tokens except proper names would be like a map the size of the country it represents. Every particular in the world could be referred to only by a unique proper name. We should gain no control over the world by means of this language; nor could it systematically disclose to us features we should not have noticed apart from it. Such a language would consist of an infinite number of unique proper names, affording us no control.

And yet, merely by introducing abstract general terms into this language the numbers of tokens we should have to commit to memory would, at once, be dramatically reduced to a finite and therefore more manageable number, and made wonderfully more powerful. Even if, let us imagine, the world were to consist of, on one hand, particulars that could be denominated exhaustively by our abstract general terms and, on the other, particulars that did not lend themselves to such classification, we should still have greatly enhanced our control over our experience. We should now have two large classes: on one hand, the *classifiable*, divisible by abstract general

[* Michael Polanyi.]

terms into many subclasses; and on the other, the *unclassifiable*, consisting of unique particulars.

At the same time, however, that our control over our prelinqual experience is enhanced by this abstraction from it and by this systematic reduction of it, the grammar, syntax, vocabulary, and etymology of our actual language greatly enrich the ways in which our opening upon time, distended between no-longer and not-yet, can be enformed.

I need only recognize how differently I would find myself being in the world, how differently I should see myself, if my language possessed no personal pronouns and had only the present indicative, compared to my actual language with its personal pronouns, the past, present, and future tenses, imperfect and perfect, in the indicative, subjunctive, imperative, and optative moods. The first is cramped; the second possesses great amplitude.

Construed in this way, language is a *theory*, an instrument for inducing a way of looking and seeing, a heuristic device of supreme power.

2/25/88

For me to know without testing whether I can, while sitting in this chair, reach the coffee table by extending my foot is a sort of knowledge which I do not usually explicitly have; and yet I rely upon it all the time in order to establish my orientation in the world of visual and motor space, whether actually or virtually.

I can have this tacit knowledge because for me to *be* a mindbody is for me always to have an unmediated apprehension of an integral formal structure: my mindbodyimage. By means of this apprehension I immediately grasp the opposition between the *here* and *there*, which refer respectively to my mindbody in this chair, on one hand, and the coffee table, on the other. But I also discern the "distance" between *here* and *there* within my own mindbodyspace, contained by its image of itself. This bodyspace could be said to be one of the senses of "the primordial here," but not the only one. As 'space' can have many uses so 'mindbodyspace' can as well.

In relying upon my immediate apprehension of the formal structure which is my mindbodyimage there is substantiated for me a kind of *motorscape* which is the condition of my ordered motility— both actual and virtual. This motorscape does the work of *theory*.

The temptation to construe the notions of mindbodyspace and

mindbodyimage as configurations in visual space—as if you could draw them on a plane surface—is so great that a warning is needed. Mindbody*space* is, at bottom, the mindbody's own intentional integration and deployment of itself within itself. The ground of my mindbodyspace is tonic with the radials of intention. Far then from this being the body's spatiality wherein it is analogous to the visual spatiality of the chair and coffee table, it is rather the *condition* for the appearance of the spatiality of these. Elsewhere I have called this mindbodyspace the primordial place.

Insofar as the mindbodyimage is the means whereby I "see" where I am in the world and provides me with the condition of ordered motility—both actual and virtual—it is a *theory*.

2/26/88

But for the work of these *theories*, serving to provide me with a "view," with a "way of seeing," inducing certain disclosures, holding and directing my attention thus and so, granting a particular form to that temporal opening at the heart of my being between no-longer and not-yet—but for these, I should be utterly lost in space and time. Indeed, so much is this the case that my bearings can become mildly disordered even when the integrity of just one of these theories loses its authority over me.

Recognizing this, we can see that ritual serves a *theoretical* function. It enables us to experience the most ordinary doings of our quotidian life as participating in a cosmic drama of "birth, copulation and death" (T. S. Eliot), of seed time and harvest, of sunrise and sunset, of hubris and reconciliation, of sin and atonement: in short, ritual enables us to see where we are in time and space—in each of their many senses—and defines for us and, in the act, reiterates to us our human identity. In this it functions as *theory*, disclosing what we would otherwise fail to notice.

The current attempt to discover practice after three centuries of Enlightenment obsession with the priority of theory, with the consequent scanting of what we *do*, is a net gain. But current discussions ignore or do not take seriously enough the logos of what we do; and this because, as with so many reformist moves, the old Enlightenment dichotomies are left unchallenged—in this case that between theory and practice. Reform consists simply in emphasizing the other side of the dichotomy after a long season of obsession with the one, and of course nothing changes. The radical move to new ground is not made: to the discovery that, in an important sense, there is no theory-neutral practice nor any practice-free theory because both are rooted in the logos of our lively mindbodies in the world. But then of course this requires no less than a systematic challenge to the whole philosophic tradition.

3/10/88

What is meant by theater of solitude? I have said elsewhere: "When I interrupt the flow of my ordinary practical activity in the world in order to reflect, I will find both myself and the objects of my curiosity presented in a certain fantasy-setting, upon some particular stage, in some singular theater both *in* which reflection is *given* and *upon* which reflection is *brought to bear.*"*

If I purpose to reflect upon the phenomena of language and, in fantasy, cast them into a theater in which, in solitude, I read silently from the printed page, these phenomena will make their exclusively visible appearance in a static setting in which neither my lively mindbody nor that of any other, and therefore neither my voice nor that of any other, can appear. It is a theater at once silent and solitary. As I read in this theater of my reflective fantasy I am alone in the static, visible world of enduring, unmoving type; a disembodied intellect in a time that is no more dynamic than that during which the letters on the printed page endure.

In this theater language is all but completely abstracted from its use. [Not completely, of course, because the words *are being read* and by a *reader.*] The words upon the printed page are taken *in themselves* to be the vectors of a disembodied and therefore impersonal meaning. At the same time, my appropriation of them as I read—a silent, static, solitary, disembodied mind—is almost equally impersonal. [I remain though, however ghostly, a *reader.*]

This abstraction can easily seduce me into tacitly believing that the concepts 'printed words' and 'reading' can have a meaning even in a conceptual universe lacking the concepts 'actual writer' and 'actual reader'—even if I do not explicitly make this claim; even if I will deny I have tacitly done so, if so accused.

[* "For Whom Is the Real Existence of Values a Problem: Or, An Attempt to Show That the Obvious Is Plausible," in *Mind, Value, and Culture: Essays in Honor of E. M. Adams,* ed. David Weissbord (Atascadero, Calif.: Ridgeview Publishing Co., 1989), 151.]

If my theory of what language is and does is derived exclusively or largely from this paradigm, it will be partial and bizarre in itself. Far weightier is the fact that, language being as fundamental to the nature of human being as it is, reliance upon this model can produce a malign effect upon our representation of the human situation.

If however the theater of reflection in which I cast the phenomena of language is one in which I read aloud to a lively audience, maintaining eye contact as I do, or if I cast them in the theater of a lively oral/aural exchange, the phenomena will by contrast appear to be richly complex and their import for philosophical anthropology very different.

For me to be able to remark *differance,** that is, the complementary simultaneous absence and presence of meaning in any given sign, it is necessary for both this *absence* and *presence* to be *in some sense* unequivocally simultaneously *present*—to me, here and now, rooted in my lively mindbody in the world, actually remarking this *differance. This* present in which I grasp the meaning of the sign as at once present and absent cannot *itself* be both present and absent—else no knot can be tied in the thread of language. The "present and absent meaning of the sign" cannot be logically reduced to "this present"; nor can it be logically reduced to "the present and absent meaning of the sign." [The fatuity that frames—imagines—this puzzle is complacently immured in the dominant visualist images.]

Whatever ambiguity or equivocation we may wish to impute to the logical force of the concept 'present' in this latter case, that force is logically heterogeneous with that of 'absence' and 'presence' when these are applied to the meaning of 'sign'. The sign and the being-remarked-by-me-as-exhibiting-*differance* no more have the same standing in the world than I and the name "William H. Poteat" have the same standing.

Thus, Derrida's claim that *all* language is shot through with *differance* is patently false. The very language in which I assert, "The meaning of a sign is simultaneously present to and absent from the sign," is, as I assert it, exempt. Nor is this riposte a mere clever logical turn lacking an anchorage in our actual being in the world. On the contrary it is designed precisely to call attention to this anchorage.

It is not likely that Derrida would have been struck by this fact, even had he conducted his inquiry into what language is and does in a theater of reflection in which he could have imagined *his own*

[* Jacques Derrida.]

words flowing from *his* pen onto the page before him *in the service* of *his asserting* the doctrine of *differance*. Had he been struck however he would have noticed that in addition to there being existing, iterable signs and codes there is also *necessarily* an *actual* "empirically determined"* writer and reader of these signs: none other than J. Derrida in the flesh, for whom the words that he writes *as* he writes are *present*, as the very condition of their being words, i.e., as the condition of their being iterable vehicles in which meaning is at once *present* and *absent*—just as these words I am just now writing can function *as words* only because the simultaneous presence and absence of their meaning is *present* to me [and to you], with, as I write, no admixture of absence, except of course when we view all of this in terms of visual models.

This *Derrida Abscondatus* is the creature of that deep spiritual investment in the idea of ourselves as discarnate Gods that underlies the thought and feeling of the last three hundred years, which we are unwilling to give up, even though its dark other side is the romantic nihilism that lies at the heart of modern sensibility.

This disclosure that there is language in use which is exempt from the blanket claim that *all* language is shot through with *differance* is no minor embarrassment for that school of deconstruction where this operates as a premise. First, it reveals the one-sidedness and artificiality of this analysis of language, making the alleged vicissitudes attending our reading and interpretation of texts that are thought to be the implicates of this analysis themselves the products of this one-sidedness.

3/11/88

Second, all this being so, the whole field of the interpretation of language and of the vicissitudes of the reading of texts will be seen to have a different center. For while it is true that the theater of solitude may make it easy for us to imagine that we are examining language in complete abstraction from any users of language—read-

[* This is no less the case when the *actual* existence of all "empirically determined" writers and readers is systematically denied in order for Derrida to make the case that cannot be coherently made. The "empirically determined" writer and reader become the necessary *conceptual* actual "empirically determined" writer and reader. See J. Derrida, "Signature Event Context," *Margins of Philosophy*, trans. Alan Bass (Chicago: University of Chicago Press, 1982), 315–16.]

ers, speakers, interpreters—so that we explicitly suppose that we can *speak* or *write* of signs, codes, iterability, *differance* without *ourselves* actually speaking and writing—a manifest impossibility—but we, by yet a further feat of abstraction, imagine that the concepts 'sign' and 'code' have a sense in a conceptual universe lacking the concepts 'writer', 'speaker', 'reader', 'interpreter'. Such a view is obviously incoherent. We however tacitly supply the conceptual conditions of the possibility of coherence, thereby making coherent what is otherwise not so, but in such a way as not to have noticed the original incoherence and also, therefore, not to have noticed that, be it ever so abstract and ghostly, there is *always* a *user* on hand. If there is necessarily *always* a *user*, then there is always a sense in which the simultaneous presence and absence of meaning in a sign is necessarily *present*, with no admixture of absence. Albeit this will not be a "present" in a dead slice of (visual) space, which of course is the sense made fashionable by literacy.

3/14/88

Now that we have discovered that the concept of a *user* is logically necessary to the conception of language as such, we begin to see that being the writer and reader of a language—even more obviously, being the speaker and hearer of one—logically cannot be an act carried out in solitude, but rather is an inherently convivial act—a universe having but a single user of a language being an incoherence. To speak, write, read, or listen is to be *present* to a language; therefore to be *virtually* in the company of all its users. A universe having but a single person is one in which a language is impossible, as Wittgenstein definitively showed in the "private language" argument.

Formulating this argument in conceptual terms will not strengthen it. Indeed, a loss will be sustained, since it will draw us away from the concrete world in which we are actually engaged in the convivial use of language and are massively confronted by the dependency of language upon a community. Yet the conceptual form does sharply focus certain features. It comes to this: the concept 'language' is meaningless apart from the concepts 'word' ('sign'), 'iterability', 'context', 'use'/'user' ('speaker'/'respondent'), 'writer'/'reader', 'speech/community', even if this last were taken to refer to but two people.

The abstract existence of this putatively timeless and placeless 'user' [even *this* 'user' occupies logical space; and *that* is *in the world*, present to my temporally distended, intentional mindbody] necessarily implies, as we have seen, the existence of at least one other user, else the spoken or written signs could not *be* signs nor any part of a code. To recognize a code for what it is is nothing less than the act of entering an actual or virtual convivial order.

The acknowledgment of this shifts to wholly new ground the focus of questions concerning our relation to texts. Occupying this new ground will call our attention to the fact that when we sit down to read and interpret a text it cannot be the case either that we are sitting nowhere or everywhere. Nor are we alone. Nine-tenths of the work of the world goes on in and proceeds from particular somewheres and particular somewhens, saved from the abyss by the fidelities of place, oblivious of the febrile nihilisms of the academy.

The vicissitudes of textual interpretation—and they are real enough—will then not seem so overwhelming. For now we can see ourselves as engaged in a conversation with our human fellows, rather than in a search for some eternal, ahistorical truth, the quest for which we now know to have been a vanity, the "loss" of which is no loss; for, after all, we have ourselves and one another, solidly grounded in history in our lively and convivial mindbodies in a real world, in the company of all of those long dead and those as yet unborn: sufficient unto the day is the evil thereof.

[In the face of relativism, these words will bring assurance only to those who have been brought to acknowledge that there is no reality more certain, more omnipresent, more valuable than a Being the nonexistence of which is inconceivable and that asseverates itself through all the quotidian sayings and doings of our convivial mindbodies, intending a world; a Being that is the absolute *arché*; the disclosures and acknowledgments of which nevertheless occur within the pretensions and retrotensions of time, itself being temporal; that is therefore, *in this sense*, "historical."

[The force and authority of *all* our uses of 'real' descend alone from this most archaic Being upon which we ubiquitously rely; even the authority by which, having taken the spoken word in its quotidian setting to be, by its "historicity," hopelessly compromised as a paradigm and vector of Being, we sublime the "eternal" written word as model of the real and as exemplary of truth.

[The failed quest for an ahistorical Truth and Reality—ahistorical in not being subject to the pretensions and retrotensions of time in their nature and in our apprehension of them—we now see to have been the price that our imaginations had to pay to have writing.

Thus were we precipitated into our thrall to the static, "eternal" written (in contrast with the dynamic, temporal spoken) word as epistemological paradigm.

[It has not been necessary that we articulate and explicitly embrace this view, though it has often been. Indeed, the force of the paradigm has been only tacitly exerted. Even Hume and Kant remained subject to the images and values of literacy, for, though denying the possibility of "metaphysical knowledge," neither shifted the ground of the debate. The form of rationality and other values that have never ceased tacitly to function in the present actuality of our oral/aural life continue, in their thought, to be suppressed.

[Yet are we not left exposed to the alleged ravages of relativism as the result of this "loss of presence"—that is, loss of an ahistorical Reality and Truth?

[There are two different senses of relativism. The first derives from the commonplace discovery that people in different times and places are given to saying and doing different things. There is little or no pathos associated with this. Indeed, we spend our whole lives almost from the moment of birth rather matter-of-factly overcoming these forms of parochialism—from learning our native language, to discovering and mitigating the otherness of our first schoolmates, to entering and appropriating other times and peoples, to indwelling the imaginations of men and women long dead, etc., etc. The limits upon the overcoming of this form of relativism are practical, not theoretical. There simply is not world enough and time. But where motivation is powerful we muster our energies to mitigate the otherness of our fathers and of our children and of our spouses—the very stuff of literature, but too concrete, too lacking in grandeur and pathos, for an Enlightenment *philosophical* theme.

[The other kind of relativism—the relativism so freighted with pathos, to whose "ravages" we feel exposed—is the child of the values and images of literacy. First we denigrate the reality and truth-bearing powers of our oral/aural life, compromised, as we suppose, by its embeddedness in the pretensions and retrotensions of time and change.

[Under the aegis of an ahistorical Truth and Reality the parochialisms of different times and places are of hardly more than tertiary philosophic interest because largely susceptible of being overcome, as desired; and, in any case, the whole realm of historical change and contingency, when viewed against the background of what we take to be an eternal Reality and Truth, is of only secondary significance. When, however, under the blows of philosophic criticism, ahistorical Truth is exposed as a chimera and we are left, so we suppose, with "only" the realities that are disclosed amid the pretensions and retrotensions of time—when, in short, we are left "only" with history, by definition devoid of an ahistoical truth—the perfectly ordinary relativism that can be overcome in practice, now viewed through the afterimage of the doctrine of an ahistorical Truth and therein showing itself destitute of any mark of truth of this kind, becomes the relativism, so heavy with pathos, that for us henceforth attests to the absence of *all* truth.

[Almost in the twinkling of an eye a benign form of historical relativism is transmogrified into its demonic form in, let us say, the writings of Nietzsche. In this view, the limits upon transcending the relativism of our position in the universe are not practical but are established a priori. Tacitly it holds that only if we could, from an eternal standpoint, transcend all parochial truths and realities as only an omniscient God can do, would we possess more than a counterfeit True and Real.

[This terrible pathos of not being God deeply afflicts us. All because the venue remains unchanged, all because after we have exposed the chimera of an eternal, ahistorical truth, we still perceive and evaluate the realm of the pretensions and retrotensions of time as from the perspective of eternity—static and changeless as the printed word is when compared with the spoken. So we think of ourselves as being left with "only" the realities and Being that are disclosed in time, and left "only" with history. The telltale presence of this "only" attests to the persistent superordinacy of the values of literacy, long after we have explicitly laid bare their pretensions. For us the use of the word 'history' continues to be governed by its relation to and contrast with 'eternity', as the oral/aural 'word' is antipathetically defined by its relation to and contrast with the printed one.

[If we can dissolve this fateful affiliation in usage, then we shall be able to imagine that history, now seen to be the setting within which a Being discloses itself that is an *other* to our operative intentions, that is ultimately oppugnant to reflection, yet in its asseverations is, like lively speech, dynamic and timeful, and whose nonexistence is inconceivable—that *history* can be the setting too of inexhaustible truths; truths that we are, in fact, continuously laying claim to in the setting of our quotidian life and so have been since time began and so shall be until the sounding of the last trump. Truth is historical because Being is historical.

[But—is this good enough? For anyone willing to accept the only world there is, nothing could be better. But do you hanker for another? Wait until the afterimage of "presence" has passed. Of course, one of the things that will pass with it is the pathos that we love so well, the nihilism of disappointed votaries of an atemporal Truth. Imagining ourselves to be gods, we lost the only world there is and can reclaim it only through an act of repentance.]

For the Greeks the particularity and transiency of our particular truths are overcome in the eternal logos; for the Hebrews they are comprehended and affirmed in the dynamic but ever faithful will of Yahweh.

3/15/88

What are the meanings of 'present' and 'absent' as these are used in the above discussion of the meaning of the sign? Obviously the two words have a multitude of uses. But it appears that their senses in the above investigation turn upon whether they function in a static or in a dynamic setting. What does this mean? To be able to say, it is necessary to examine the notion of time in the context of both orality and literacy.

The time within which our spoken words unfold in the oral/aural setting is different from the time of the endurance of *relatively* unchanging objects in visual space. Here objects appear as simultaneously co-present to vision—*as we have*, in this tradition, *described vision*, and as this description *functions in our reflection*. In our reflected articulations, this relatively static background of objects, enduring in a time that is intimately associated with the visual space in which these objects are co-present, is sharply in contrast with the time within which our spoken words dynamically unfold in relative independence of their static spatial background, and are both *present with* and *absent from* one another in oral/aural time as words are that precede and succeed one another in this time. Of course, in the unreflected actuality of our lively, intentional mindbodies these times cohere: both the relatively static time of objects enduring in visual space and the relatively fleeting time of a succession of spoken and heard words in the time of oral/aural reciprocity.

Printed words, in contrast with those of lively speech, then, endure in visual space. They do not come into being and pass out of being in that time in which our spoken words appear, are heard, and then are heard no more.

In these two sharply divergent cases the forces of the words *'presence'* and *'absence'* are very different. In a discourse dominated by images drawn from the seeing of printed words in visual space *'present'* will mean "in view in visual space" or "in sight"; *'absent'* will therefore mean "out of sight," not before us in visual space. In a discourse dominated by images drawn from the world of dynamic oral/aural time, *'present'* will mean something like *actual*, as the A theme in a sonata may be said to be actual when the entire theme has been stated; and *'absent'* will mean *potential* as the B theme may be said to be until it has been stated. Or, another illustration, *'present'* will mean *actual* as those words are actual that I have just spoken and that now appear in the oral/aural world; and *'absent'* will mean potential as those words are potential that you and I both anticipate that I am on the point of speaking.

In his argument to *differance* as the condition of iterability, hence of signs and codes, Derrida is oblivious of the above distinction. This does not seriously flaw his analysis of language narrowly conceived and as far as it goes—which, we have seen, is very narrow and not far enough by a great deal. But most of the time he draws his conception of absence from the visualist sense, delivering his views from obvious incoherence for himself by tacitly supplying the necessary correctives.

Now, to *sight alone*—and of course it is never alone except in our partial, reflected accounts, heavily biased by our literacy—if anything is "out of sight" it has *completely* disappeared from *sight*. A radical break occurs: *to sight alone*, to exist is to be seen, not to be seen is not to exist. It was out of such an imaginative picture that Descartes declared the world to be created anew in every instant. And it was on these same premises that that arch-Cartesian, J.-P. Sartre, claimed that man has to choose himself into existence in every instant. Anything else would be bad faith.

It is this conception of *absence* (from sight alone) that underlies Derrida's analysis of *differance*—a hardly controversial claim about the condition for the possibility of language—which is the source in his writings of the pathos of loss, and, in its most radical forms, of romantic nihilism.

3/17/88

It is a grave temptation for me to imagine that the space and time within which my mindbody's intentional integration and self-deployment are accomplished, in both its specific and its ongoing activity of maintaining itself in unity, is the space and time within which I move from point A to point B in this room.

Not so. My mindbody is the absolutely radical and prior—at the root of and antecedent to absolutely everything (!)—*here* and *now*: *the primordial place*; whence all times and spaces are pretended; that every time and space retrotends. There being this place is not the *condition* of my mindbodily integrity; it *is* this integrity.

Are, then, all these derivative times and spaces unreal? Certainly not; just derivative. They are as real, even if not as radical, as that from which they derive: our sentient, motile, oriented, and convivial mindbodies in the world.

3/24/88

For me to be able to judge that the concept 'language' is meaningless apart from the concepts 'word', 'iterability', 'user', 'speech-community' is for me to "have" these concepts, that is, to know how to use these words, to be able to recognize the sorts of contexts in which they typically play their roles, to know how their uses are mutually implicative, how they require one another. For me to claim to *know* how to use them is of course for me to posit *usage*. I cannot, after all, be said to *know* how to use 'snerk'. It obeys no rules, is appropriate in some contexts, inappropriate in others. All these powers of discrimination and judgment I cultivated as, in the course of time, I acquired a native language within the mindbodily convivium of native speakers.

Even, then, for me, however abstractly, to speak of the concept 'concept', either *viva voce* or in writing, is for me to trade upon my own *presently actual* mindbodily existence in the world and my own *actual* history as a competent user of language—which is to say, a "possessor" of concepts, a present practitioner of a skill—as the basis of my understanding of a usage. And anyone who writes for me to read of the concept 'concept' will have traded upon his or her own then presently actual existence and history, as a competent user of language. This means of course that no matter how alienated it may be in time and space from a presently actual feat of writing, the appearance of the concept 'concept' will have necessitated and therefore will necessarily imply the existence of actual users, of usage, contexts, a speech-community, etc.

What an incredibly tortured way to declare the obvious: that for there to be a concept of 'concept' there must either now be or once have been *actual* users of the word 'concept'; that for there to be 'logical entailment' there must now be or once have been persons for whom this holds; that for there to be meaning there must be those to whom meaning appears as such.

Why have I done this? Why do I find myself going to these absurd lengths? Above, in the course of my conceptual argument against Derrida, referring to the "abstract existence of this putatively timeless and placeless 'user,'" I wrote: "Even *this* 'user' occupies logical space; and *that* is *in the world*, present to my temporally distended, intentional mindbody." Reading this over, I am startled to realize that I was somehow going against the grain of my own imagination, as I supposed, "boldly" claiming that even the "abstract existence of a putatively timeless and placeless ['merely conceptual'] 'user'" is *existentially* dependent upon my "temporally distended, intentional mindbody" [N.B.! This is not to be absent-mindedly assimilated to "mind-dependent" as the tradition I am now attacking tempts me to do]. What made me suppose that this needed saying? Against what inertia in myself was I working?

I believe it is my tacit assumption—this is too strong a word, it is more a vague feeling—that concepts are mental entities; that minds are *essentially* what they are quite independently of what are taken to be their "contingent" carnal embodiments; that therefore concepts are not *necessarily* but only *contingently* dependent upon the existence of actual speakers; that they are, in other words, *in a sense*, timeless and placeless.

To put these attitudes into words is to make it difficult to imagine anyone having them. Yet the power of their effect in our imaginations *before articulation* is not less, but rather more, by reason of their vagueness. I believe these tacit assumptions are more widely pervasive in the ethos of our philosophic tradition than is suspected. I do not of course mean the explicit formulations of the mental/physical dualisms and the explicit philosophical colloquies which have revolved about them. These are easily identified and easily brought under criticism at the explicit level. The motifs to which I refer operate in subtler ways. In fact, they have come to the surface here for me for the first time, as I undertake to deconstruct my own imagination, notwithstanding my lifelong quarrels with the explicit dualisms of our tradition, and even with many of its tacit forms. It was against this in myself that I wrote in making my "bold" claim.

Our sense seems to be that if we drive a broad enough wedge between the concept of an "empirical user" and the concept of a mere conceptual user, we can then imagine that the latter—and, of course, all concepts as compared to "empirical entities"—will be that curious kind of entity that is *no* entity, namely one that enjoys an exemption from being in the world, subject to its conditions.

3/25/88

When all is said and done, we arrive at this summary conclusion: the *existence* of concepts, which is to say, the existence of usages, and the *having* of concepts, that is, the knowing how to *observe* usages, are as inextricably entangled in the warp and weave of the actual world of our senses, in, that is, the so-called empirical world, as is the very language we speak and write; and this because they *are* the language we speak and write. Concepts therefore have no other existence than this. And the grammar and syntax of the language we speak and write are rooted in and derived from the "grammar" and "syntax" of our mindbodies.

The presumptively sharp dichotomy between "the conceptual" and "the empirical"—which lay at the root of the conclusion that issued above in my "bold" denial of the timelessness and placelessness of concepts—can no longer hold. What survives is a distinction between, on one hand, the contemplation of usages, prescinded from any actual use, and, on the other, the actual, concrete use of a word in a context. Even this can have but limited employment.

My sentient, oriented, motile mindbody is continuously engaged in the activity of fashioning a coherent world out of the materials at hand—motifs, theories (in the above sense), verbal assertions, gestures—myths, histories, conversations, narratives, poems, metaphors, general theories of the physical universe, architecture, string quartets, the drama of the weather, the coming of night, the passing expression on your face, etc., etc.—among which it is quite impossible to fashion coherence explicitly, from a detached point of view, since to such a point of view none exists. Or can be made to appear to exist only because we surreptitiously supply our own mindbody wherein alone they can cohere. This is one of the things I mean when I say that the mindbody is the ubiquitous ground of meaning and meaning-discernment. *Doing* all of this and *being* what it is are one and the same. Of course, by tacitly completing a theory of language acquisition such as Chomsky's or tacitly correcting a theory such as B. F. Skinner's their mindbodies make two theories which are incoherent appear plausible to their authors. And the irony is—as it is of the Enlightenment's grip upon our imaginations across the board—that there is nothing in the theories of these two to account for the way their incoherent theories are made to seem plausible to them.

3/30/88

Of course, the Enlightenment has intimidated us with its impeachment of myths, all the while preserving and fashioning myths of its own. Yet, here again the potency of our unarticulated, vague feelings becomes evident. Long after we have become accustomed to reiterating our charge against the Enlightenment at the explicit level, we discover ourselves living under the press of our vague feelings that its views of myth are correct. We are immured in our unresolved, affective evaluations.

Above I have written ". . . our matter-of-fact references to the past and to the future . . . derive their authority and indubitability from their grounding in our primitive worldliness prior to our alienation from it in reflection. It is in this primitive worldliness that the weight and authority of myth are founded."

Reading this over months after writing it, the very mention of the word 'myth' alerts in me those unresolved feelings of skepticism. There can be little quarrel over the matter-of-fact references to the (what we sometimes think of as the no longer existing) past and the (not yet existing) future, being grounded in our primitive worldliness. This angle of vision will yield a different and less abstract way of thinking about the past and future by *locating* that thinking in our actual *uses* of the past and future tenses, and by grounding these usages in the authority of our primitive worldliness. But myths! Grounding *them* in this primitive worldliness? Highly dubious special pleading! I know well enough about my references to the past and future, have no doubts about their efficacy and authority in my quotidian life. But *myths*? I know nothing of these in that life. They are not grounded there as my references to the past and future are. What is the source of the ambivalence in me that inclines me to retreat from the position I have articulated?

First, when I think about myth, child of Enlightenment that I am, I am very likely to think as an anthropologist; that is, I take myself to be trying to understand a thing as alien to my own mode of being in the world as is another culture. Already I regard it as something peculiarly problematic; more problematic than the strange language of this alien culture.

3/31/88

I, after all, know intimately what a language is. But as to myths, I have everything yet to learn. So I think to myself, in my posture as Enlightenment anthropologist student of the "strange" phenomenon of myth. [All this notwithstanding that the putatively "strange" phenomenon is itself in fact an invention of the *Enlightenment* myth.] There are still residues of this in isolated pockets of *this* (i.e., modern Western) culture, I can see. Myths are for me, as anthropologist, interesting, but strange—something I investigate from outside, but not something of a sort I might myself conceivably dwell in.

Second, this anthropological perspective prevents me from getting in touch with the actual grain of my life as I live it, where the "myths" that enform the shape of that life are authoritatively embedded. Wherever memory and hope make their appearance in the temporal structures of my life, there are myths, or fragments of myths. And these are not just about the no-longer and the not-yet. They are about *now* in its fullness and depth.

Looking at myth from the kind of anthropological perspective I have imagined is analogous to looking at sensory experience from the standpoint of the *psychology* of sense perception in the hope that through this you can enter and understand the world of our senses.

The mythical "component" of my world has the same standing, is as little, in principle, problematic as is the "component" of my sense experience of the world. [My world is, after all, not made up *of components*.] They both have their authority for me because they are both grounded in the one matrix of all meaning and meaning-discernment—my lively mindbody. If the present were *only* present, if it were not given depth and fecundity by memory and hope, we could not be human.

When I wrote above that "it is in this primitive worldliness that the weight and authority of myth are grounded," I knew whereof I spoke. It was only when I read this over later, as an "anthropologist," that I was made to distrust myself.

4/4/88

Philosophical idealism gets its traction from the curious (false) assumption that the act of *conceiving* of 'concept', 'percept', 'mind', 'body', etc., is a *mental* event strictly *mind-dependent*. Therefore one has the *mental* entity, 'concept', and the mental act, "thinking-of-concept": ergo, idealism. Even when an idealist seeks to catch this "mind-dependent" event in the act, he systematically removes himself, his *mindbodily activity in the act of reflecting,* in order to observe what the act is; forgetting his own mindbodily being, he depicts his reflective act as (merely) *mental.* Idealism systematically annuls the datum that is its own refutation.

[If the issue in the debate over foundationalism/anti-foundationalism is understood to be the question "Is the hierarchy of our thought and judgment finally grounded in something that stands fast?" then the attempt to formulate the problem confronts a paradox at the outset. For it assumes that all of the elements that bear upon the question lie open to our detached and lucid reflection, *even though* an acritical, unreflected, and therefore heterogeneous act of "thinking" and "judging" has been antecedently laid down as the very condition of such an articulation.

[To this antecedent act of "thinking" and "judging," from which issues the lucidly formulated foundationalist/anti-foundationalist problematic, the question Is this antecedent act grounded or ungrounded? is neither being applied *in fact,* nor is it in principle possible of application, save on pain of an infinite regress. The question is systematically put out of play. At each successive stage of such a regress I will be relying once again upon "thought" and "judgment" already acritically at work. Between myself and my reliance upon this "thought" and "judgment" there is no logical space for the question of foundations to arise; just as between the *words* I am asserting and my *assertion* of them there is no such space. In a "world" defined by an infinite regress nothing could *be,* nothing could be *said* or *done.* But things *are,* and they *are* said and done; therefore the world does not have the character of an infinite regress. It is *there;* and inescapably there; except perhaps to chronic philosophical triflers.

[The relation I have, then, to the formulation of the problematic of foundationalism/anti-foundationalism is of a different logical order from that I have to the "thought" and "judgment" of which it is the issue. One is logically heterogeneous vis-à-vis the other.

[The acritical, antecedent thought that issues in the lucid problematic is grounded in that radix of all meaning and meaning-discernment: our sentient, oriented, motile, convivial mindbodies.

[This irreducible hierarchy of logico-ontological levels shows itself ubiquitously in the structures of our form of life; and in the integrity of the actual world in which we ingenuously and ineluctably live.

[Increasingly intellectuals, displaced from themselves by the ravages of the ideology of "ideology," seem ontologically incapable of *seriousness*: the concept of responsibility has lost its force among them. When this becomes a norm against which dissent is impossible—as may already have happened in the academy—humane letters, their creation and their study, will be at an end. For their subject matter has at bottom always been nothing other than the representation of the ways that human beings succeed and fail at assuming responsibility, which is to say, at being human.

[For example, when advocates of anti-foundationalism seek to defend themselves against their critics they slip into a theater of reflection that can only be described as logocentric.

[Within this imaginative structure that operates at their backs words are represented as alienated from *use*; abstracted from their role as actual vectors of responsible utterance—whether spoken or written—apart from which "words" can be no more than sounds or inscribed shapes. This logocentrism is the habit of depicting language, its tokens, logical grammar, syntax, and rhetorical strategies as if they were utterly discarnate. Yielding completely to the logical demands of this picture—and it's only common sense that inhibits our doing so—entails that there can *be* no logical grammar, syntax, semantics, or rhetoric governing these—what shall we call them?—they would not be "words."

[Every speaker (writer) *as speaking* (writing) and as *personally owning* his or her own words always acritically and unconditionally occupies the *actual*, not a merely possible, infinitely commutable, world—whatever the contingencies and relativities that necessarily attend *every* mode of dwelling there, however fungible that mode in that actual world may appear to be when contemplated by thought that has been abstracted from this world. If this were not so, the doctrine of anti-foundationalism could not be said. Nor indeed could anything else.

[To be sure, the above argument has little chance of gaining traction with those to whom it is directed; for the condition of its doing so is the deconstruction of their logocentrism, the overcoming of their impulse in reflection to burke responsibility for their own uttered words. This impulse is deeply rooted in a whole *Weltanschauung* that has for centuries increasingly wrought attrition upon the very concept 'responsibility'.

[If however the anti-foundationalists' view is, as I have claimed, systematically incoherent, how is it kept afloat? Why, its protagonists, unwittingly, abandon the images in the logocentric theater of reflection in favor of those that enform our ordinary practice of speaking and writing. It is here of course, in varying ways, that we are *accountable* for what we say, are taken to be *serious*, even in order that we may at times be less than fully so. By this logical sleight-of-hand is coherence gained for views that otherwise are wholly without it. Neither the fact nor the philosophic import of these moves is acknowledged.]

4/7/88

The existential *is* expresses not only existence, but value and authority; albeit as its use and application are more remote from *its* ground and authority, *viz.*, the Being the nonexistence and disvalue of which is inconceivable, its concrete force as value and authority is attenuated.

This reflection is prompted by my observation that the closer I come in reflection to the ground of reflection, namely to my mind-body in its immediacy, the less tenable becomes the distinction between facts and values until at last it becomes quite untenable.

The illusion of value-free discourse—discourse, that is to say, whose meaning is not seen to be derivative of and whose present authority is not recognized as alone descending from their ground in our mindbodily being in the world, and that therefore is imagined to be the perfect reflective medium of a discarnate mind—is the creature of *mathesis universalis*, a language without verbs, tenses, demonstratives, or personal pronouns.

5/19/88

At bottom it was Descartes who gave us "Turing's man"—a conception of ourselves as discarnate logic machines who "process information," crunch numbers, store and retrieve data, who wait in hope for the day when artificial intelligence not only will surpass our powers, but will exhaustively simulate thought, devise programs, and even make main-frame computers of its own design. As we more and more come to dwell in these models some of our actual powers atrophy and a whole stratum of human reality is repressed—with what long-term effects we can only guess.

Whatever the regnant interpretation of science at a given moment in the history of modernity, two beliefs may be said to have dominated its practice: the belief that to understand is to reduce and that to explain is to devise a causal theory. These beliefs have governed the conditions in which in our soberest moments we have permitted ourselves to make the claim "I know." Uses of the verb "to know" not meeting this putatively sole, truly exacting, test of epistemological probity—"true exactitude," after all, is itself question-beggingly defined by these beliefs—have been banished or at least have become the occasion of embarrassment in genteel philosophical circles.

Taking this model of the practice of science as a norm, one will have to say that there can be a *science* of our cognitive efforts that misfire, but no *science*, in the above sense, of our cognitive feats that succeed. For to appreciate what is involved in a successful feat of knowing we shall have to accredit uses of the verb "to know" and learn to practice modes of paying attention long officially in dispute in modernity.

For example, we shall have to recognize that to *describe* a phenomenon accurately—as it ingenuously presents itself, unreduced and unexplained—is truly a way of *understanding* this phenomenon. [It might be concluded from this too cryptic remark that I assume that the language of such a description would be presuppositionless. Obviously not. It can be claimed however that "ordinary language," presuppositionful as it assuredly is, is less removed from the way the world presents itself to our common sense than is the language of reductionistic and causally explanatory science, since this language has the authority of being the one we speak most of the time about what we know most intimately; and therefore is the best medium of *another, real* mode of knowing.] This is the mode of coming to understand appropriate to things and events that disappear when they are subject to conceptual reduction or causal explanatory theory. [It is worth observing *en passant* that, if we could by some science-fictional legerdemain conceptually represent to ourselves *in an instant* the whole commonsense world that is represented to us *piecemeal* in our reductionistic and causally explanatory science, that ordinary world in its fullness would vanish.] A successful cognitive feat is just such a phenomenon. The *essential* nature of our acts of coming to know can be apprehended only in their actual setting in our lively mindbodies in *their* setting in our quotidian practice.

One of the aspirations of computer science is to devise an artificial intelligence that can exactly simulate human intelligence—the assumption being that, if we can produce artificial "human" intelligence, we shall then have come fully to understand natural intelligence.

The use of the adjective 'artificial' seems tacitly to concede that any such intelligence is the progeny—in each of several senses—of the "natural" intelligence of actual men and women; and the use of the verb 'simulate' implies that it is not, after all, quite the real thing—suggesting that a question as to the philosophic import of these differences needs asking.

Fully to understand these issues would require an examination and critique of the models of inquiry and of knowing that gained ascendancy with the rise of science and technology. One can however ask what are the logical—as opposed to the merely technical—limits upon the fulfillment of these aspirations; and why we seem inclined, our instinctive resistance to the contrary notwithstanding, to believe that there are none.

Of course, the quest for a fully adequate artificial simulation of the powers of human intelligence founders, in the end, upon an insuperable barrier—as self-evident to our common sense as it is shocking to our feverish hope of understanding all by reducing all—quite simply, I and my intelligence are alive, the computer is not. Everyone of course knows this. We need to take it seriously.

5/23/88

A signal disanalogy between me and a computer: let me begin here. But first a warning. Some of the enthusiasts for artificial intelligence will declare that these disanalogies have no bearing at all upon the fundamental questions of their inquiry; and that, in any case, these disanalogies are self-evident and can safely be ignored. What happens here is this: the disanalogies which are asserted to be self-evident are ignored when they ought to be made *explicit*; yet they are *tacitly* conceded in order to render the aspirations to an exhaustive model of human intelligence coherent, when without this concession it could not be. The net result is that while the quest for higher and higher modes of simulation proceeds without serious impediments—any systematic incoherence resulting from the disanalogies being systematically corrected by our tacit demand for coherence—philosophical anthropology is profoundly warped because the disanalogies are never taken seriously in an *explicit* way. The extent to which an artificial intelligence cannot overcome those disanalogies—and is taken to be the paradigm of human being—is the extent to which we will be represented as discarnate logic-machines in the tacit philosophical anthropology regnant in this culture.

Now to a signal disanalogy between me and a computer.

A computer cannot, as I do, use the pronoun in the first-person singular, nominative case to make a reference to itself. It will of course be rejoined that a computer could be programmed in such a way that if I were to type into it the question, "Who put the overalls in Mrs. Murphy's chowder?" it would be able to print out on its screen, "I did"; and this might be taken to be an instance of genuine "self-reference."

But observe. When *I* make a reference to myself by means of the first-person pronoun, I not only denominate myself *for you* as "the one who did it," I distinguish myself *for myself* from all the worldly others that I am not. I am not merely distinguishing "the speaker" from all other speakers; nor *this* agent from all other agents; nor *this* (my) place in space and time from all others. Rather I am *for myself*, no less than for you, distinguishing from all others this (my) temporally distended mindbodily person to whom the first-person pronoun reflexively refers as I use it. In using it—of course, necessarily—of myself I *take* this surrogate name as *mine*, even as I have *taken* my proper name. To have a name (or a surrogate name) as men and women do is not just to have been *given* a name as a star or a mountain or a disease is given one; or as the name "Hal" was given to the computer in the movie *2001*. To have a name as you and I do is to *take* a name. Nor is taking a name reducible to the mere saying (printing out) of the words, "my name is William H. Poteat." This difference between being given a name and taking a name is self-evident to common sense—though the impulse to deny what common sense finds irresistible is great in the ethos of modernity.

If, in face of this imperious demand, I momentarily yield and begin to imagine that, after all, "I" as "used" by a computer is indistinguishable from *my* use of I—that *it* "uses" "I" to distinguish "itself" for itself from other "speakers," etc.—how will I have placated the ingenuous demands of common sense to the contrary? The answer is that I will have set 'I', 'use', 'itself', and 'speaker', as applied to the computer, into the logico-grammatical context that they occupy when used in my exchanges with you and other ordinary speakers of our language. In short, to avoid offense to common sense I surreptitiously supply the omnipresent stage setting of the ordinary conversations we have with one another, *as if it were native to my "conversations" with a computer*, which of course it is not.

In these logico-grammatical equivocations, I impute to the computer powers that belong only to you and me. And to keep my footing as I have worked my way through the conceptual thicket above I have routinely placed scare-quotes around "I," "use," "itself," and "speaker" to remind myself and you that their logical force was *not* that which they enjoy in ordinary discourse.

When therefore I read 'I' off the computer screen, if I take the logical force of this 'I' to be identical with its force as I use it to refer to myself, it will be because I will have imputed to it a worldly context such as would obtain if *you* were, in my presence, to use 'I' to refer to yourself. And what is this worldly context? Well, one of the marks of worldliness is for there to be between you and me, and between us and all the others, that which is common to us all, in the midst of which *we each perceive ouselves to be both distinct from and with others*. I *provide* a worldly context for this computer-I in my assumption that *its* "I" is addressed to a "you" (whom *I* know as "I" and "me") that is *for it* existentially *over against it* (and not merely in the way that the grammatical second person is *grammatically* over against the first person).

5/24/88

Here I have placated the demands of common sense by imagining—what is of course not the case—that I am *for* the computer-I (which, even here, common sense rebels at addressing as "you") in exactly the same way that I am *for you*. In fact, the computer cannot know *me* as "you" (known also to myself as "I") as *you* know me as "you," because between it and me there is in fact no world.

Nor, of course, is it less disingenuous for me tacitly to assume that I am *for* the computer-I as I am *for you*. This is conceivable only if we take it that the computer-I is *for itself* as *you* are *for yourself*, as the condition of my being for you in the way we commonsensically take for granted.

All these incoherences we tacitly resolve by providing the stage setting of a lively, conscious person with whom we are face to face when in fact none such exists. Thus can we grimly obey with minimum discomfort the injunction, "Reduce in order to understand."

Consciousness requires at any given moment a center and a periphery that are dialectically [and I wish to have felt the full force of the metaphor of a *lively* oral/aural exchange that is implicated in the word 'dialectically'] in pretensive and retrotensive communication with each other. How do I know this? I know it by dwelling directly in the actual structure of my own consciousness—that is to say, in the structure of my lively, sentient, and oriented mindbody. This tensive gestalt enforms the whole range of my conscious life and forces itself upon me as the simplest condition of such life. Any putative representation less complex than this is too simple—which, of course, the computer model precisely is.

This center and periphery in their most radical manifestations, which is the form of interest to us here, are not loci within the system of my body as organism—not, on the one hand, my head and trunk, say, and my skin, on the other; not my brain and central nervous system as over against the afferent and efferent nerves that communicate with my "outside." It is rather that, for example, at a given moment the nail that I am in that moment driving with a hammer can be construed to be the frontier at which my *mindbody* meets the world, and my center will be the mindbodily coherence that sustains and that I "perceive" as sustaining this act. Or, an alternative example, my periphery may be the mindbodily recollection of an event in my boyhood in China in 1925 and my center will be my mindbodily act of writing of this time to a friend today. Consciousness may thus have a very narrow focus or be virtually infinite in scope. But center and periphery are always moments in my mindbodily life that have this irreducibly tonic relation to one another. To lose consciousness is precisely to have this tonic bond dissolve.

Animals (including of course ourselves) are sentient, as opposed to merely having sense data, because they are conscious. But, we think, could we not devise a computer that would be capable of sensory experience; by supplying it, for example, with artificial sensors? And the answer is, no—a logical, not a mere technical, impossibility. The repertoire of concepts by means of which we appropriately think of computers does not include those concepts necessary for a faithful analysis of our own actual sensory experience of the world—*except to the extent to which we illicitly impute them to this repertoire*, as, we have seen above, we do. If we are *conceptually strict*, we cannot imagine a computer that has sensory experience. Our own sensory experience, after all, is not of *this* color, and then *that* shape, and then *this* tone. "These" are always apprehended within the intentional fabric of our mindbodies as consciousness within a world.

The relation between a source or medium of "sense data" at a "periphery," on one hand, and a "center" at which these are "received," on the other—the scare-quotes are to remind us that this is a popular but bogus account that seems to fit the computer case, but that bears no relation to the reality of human sensory experience—is *not* at every moment dialectically pretensive and retrotensive, but rather is simply linear: lacking the *tone* that my mindbody possesses as a mark of being alive and as the condition of the capacity, for example, to hear tones and melodies composed of tones. In hearing a melody I don't, after all, hear A *and then* hear B *and then* hear C. I can hear a melody *as melody* only because I hear A pretending B and B retrotending A.

No servomechanism, however sophisticated, no electronic system of loops and reciprocating feedback channels, however redundant, can exactly simulate the irreducible tonicity of a single living cell. In all of the former there is but the flat, unilateral, unidirectional passage from the "periphery" to the "center," from the "center" to the "periphery"; not the lively pretension/retrotension that holds between center and periphery characterizing the tone of a living cell and of consciousness.

5/25/88

As we have seen, the concept of a center requires its co-implicate, the periphery. It makes as little sense to speak of a center and a periphery of a computer's program as to speak of center and periphery in a universe that is an infinite sphere. These notions can have standing only where the ego-centric particulars "here" and "now" and "there" and "then" have a specific existential reference. Being worldless, the computer's program, taken strictly in itself, is without a meaning for "here" or "there." A computer cannot be made to simulate recognizing that it *has* a program in the sense in which I can recognize that I command the use of a language.

When I undertake to think of its program as being the center of a computer, I find I can do this only by thinking that its program stands to *it* as its program would stand to me, if it were mine. In other words, it can be thought to have a center only as an imaginative derivation of my own immediate sense of existential centeredness. Only in this way can this kind of talk about computers gain some traction.

All of the sciences that stand under the umbrella of "cognitive science" [it is misleading to characterize them as "subordinate," for this suggests that their conceptual relations with each other are logically hierarchical and have been worked through. They have not. But then they need not be in order to do their several jobs. The absence of an explicit hierarchy is overcome by their being brought into conjunction and order in the *practice* of those who profess them, in the background of which practice are, ubiquitously, the ground of all meaning and meaning-discernment, their sentient and oriented mindbodies]—molecular biology, neuro-anatomy, neurology, cybernetics, linguistics/semiotics, psychology, epistemology—can be made to yield a full representation of a cognition, i.e., a person actually coming to know something in the ordinary world, only if a "cognitive scientist" is seen as *himself* coming to know something, namely, in the act of integrating all of the realities that are the subject matter of these sciences to the comprehensive entity that is his own cognitive act, grasped from within; and who acknowledges, in doing so, that this act cannot be reduced to its constituent particulars without incoherency.

This is a complicated way of saying that the various scientists operating under the umbrella of cognitive science in principle explicitly—and within strict limits, justifiably—ignore themselves as the actual knowers of what they know, while they rescue their enterprise from incoherency by tacitly reintroducing into it themselves as the knowers of what they know.

5/26/88

It is our commonsensical experience of knowing what we know in our most quotidian doings that has first evoked our interest in cognition, it is this that continues to sustain it, and it is these ubiquitous cognitive acts that at once inescapably accompany and systematically elude all our investigations of them. It is these unreduced acts of knowing and judging that we know in the setting of our ordinary doings that are the *ultimate* subject of a "science" of cognition. The method for their study therefore will have to be a reflexive phenomenology—that is, a systematic description, in ordinary rather than in an artificially contrived language, of our feats of coming to know, reflexively grasped from within as they actually unfold in time. Not an easy task, since in the intellectual environment where to understand is in principle to reduce and to explain is to devise a causal theory—both of which alienate us from our own actual feats of knowing—a mere description such as this will compete among us most unevenly for serious attention.

Yet the concept of "an actual person coming to know something" does not, of course, appear in the conceptual repertoire of any of the cognitive sciences—except as surreptitiously supplied in response to the exigent demand for coherence that can be met only by this conceptual sleight-of-hand.

But what, after all, is the harm in this? The harm is to philosophical anthropology, to our conception of ourselves as incarnate spirits that is implicit in this tacit reductionism.

What purposes then do these sciences serve, if they do not enable us to apprehend the roots of cognition in its irreducibility—that is, of course, apart from the disinterested pleasure they give in showing us, for example, the wonder of the central nervous system?

You cannot explain how a machine achieves its mechanical telos in terms of the laws of physics and chemistry. This requires an appeal to the operational principles of machines.*

5/27/88

The concept 'purpose' and therefore the concepts 'succeed' and 'fail' are no part of the conceptual repertoire required for the understanding of chemical-physical entities; only on the level of machines and their operational principles are they required. When a machine breaks down, it can no longer achieve its end. It is then that we will invoke a physico-chemical explanation of its failure: "metal fatigue"—essential knowledge for mechanics and designers of machines.

By the same argument it is clear that you cannot give a neurophysiological explanation of how a person successfully performs a cognitive act, since for this we require the concepts 'consciousness', 'sentience', 'world', 'intention'—essentially in their commonsense uses—and these are not in the neurophysiological repertoire. Yet a neurophysiological explanation is at hand when "a man mistakes his wife for a hat." We look for a lesion in the central nervous system.

5/30/88

As you cannot derive the concept of a machine from an inventory of its physico-chemically defined particulars, so you cannot derive the

[* Michael Polanyi.]

concept of an act of cognition in its fullness from a detailing of its neurological ones.

The several sciences under the umbrella of cognitive science, then, cannot fully disclose, strictly on their own terms, how our cognitive acts succeed, and therefore they cannot tell us *what they are;* but they can show us what has gone awry when they fail—by no means a small thing, if therapy is what is required.

And there is no escape for the cognitive scientist from this irreducible, intransigent reality that is himself at the center of his own act of knowing, no matter how assiduously he attempts to analyze and reduce even *this* act by applying to it the categories of the several sciences. The cognitive act by which he makes these applications to and judgments about his acts systematically eludes this analysis. To the cognitive acts of others and even of himself—except the very one in which he is now engaged—he can achieve a measure of detachment. The one in which he is *now* engaged however systematically eludes his own detached analysis.

And what is obscured in this detached analysis? The recognition that his every cognitive act is set within the worldly sentience, motility, and orientation toward meaning and value of his unreflected mindbody.

[What is, by default, overlooked in our reflections on the powers of computers and on their prospects as exhaustive models of human intelligence is the fact that they (logically) cannot embody and express *in themselves* that the data they contain is at once derived *from* and *bears upon* the world of common sense. The computer's own internal logic is worldless and therefore systematically abstracts itself from the actual world. The code of the computer lacks natural language's resources—the demonstratives 'this' and 'that', for example—for making references to an *actual,* as opposed to a merely logically possible, world. To be sure, given its purposes, there is no reason that it should be otherwise; indeed, given its purposes, it could *not* be otherwise. But we need to wonder whether this is a shortcoming we can tolerate in a putatively exhaustive model of human intelligence.]

The animus of my critique of a reduced and causally explanatory account of cognition derives not from an intrinsic interest in this, but rather from a concern with yet another instance of the deepgoing impulse toward reductionism in the modern imagination. To be human is to be an incarnate spirit. Any account of human being that does not systematically depict and ingeminate this most rudimental truth about us is a philosophy *manqué.* My lively mindbody *as consciousness* is at once the condition of the possibility of and the intentional ground for my every cognitive act.

In this culture we are so habituated to reducing in order to understand and so accustomed, too, to offsetting the incoherence of doing this by tacitly correcting for it that we are quite ingenuously puzzled or defensive if an explicit charge to this effect is made against us.

5/31/88

The actual *uttering* of the Latin words *cogito ergo sum* has more authority as an attestation of my existence than the bedrock inference that is expressed in these uttered words. Descartes, as he utters *cogito ergo sum*, is necessarily committal, acritical in his relation to his words. *As he uses these very words*, it is *logically impossible* for him to *imagine* that it is a matter wholly indifferent whether he uses *these* words or others. In no sense are they "mere conventions." We have—because it deeply satisfies our vanity to do so—leapt over this inconvenient stumbling block. The history of modern philosophy is the history of this bad faith.

6/6/88

Whence our conception of the absolutely contingent, defined as that which is oppugnant to *all* antecedent meaning—difficult, really impossible, for us coherently to imagine, bound, as it must be, to the necessary ground of all meaning and meaning-discernment? The source of the idea of the "contingent" is nothing other than the radical underivability of my every act of speaking in my own name, when this act has been wholly prescinded from the rich, concrete context in which it always occurs—indeed, prescinded from *any* context whatsoever, save that context of *being oppugnant* to any context. And this power to speak in my own name, always given in the fabric of my intentional mindbodily life in all its density—arising *in* and subject *to* the conditions of, though not derivable *from*, or explicable *by*, this setting—is itself the absolutely irreducible and underived bedrock of human being. This is what we mean by the phrase "conditioned freedom." Freedom, as this power to take responsibility for myself within the setting of my mindbodily life, subject to all its own primordial ordinations, to the otherness of the ordered world and the styles and structures of my culture, far from being a mere "moral certainty," required to secure the authority of our moral sensibility, as Kant seems to have thought, is rather itself the *conditio sine qua non*, the ground and source of that sensibility.

This ubiquitous *fact* of human freedom, manifest in all the ways in which I take the world upon myself as my own—in feats, both tacit and explicit, of speaking, judging, making truth-claims with universal intent, forming for myself a conception of the nature of things, accepting responsibility for all of these as mine—is antecedent to any question concerning the *possibility* of human freedom. A quite new relationship between the exercise of my freedom as taking responsibility and the worldly and historical setting in which it *always* necessarily occurs can now be seen. The exercise and therefore the possibility of my freedom are not oppugnant to worldly and historical conditions, but rather *require* them. This renders moot a good deal of the debate over human freedom. And it takes the sting out of reductive, Marxist criticism.

6/20/88

Because of its radical, through-and-through intentionality, my lively mindbodily being in the world is shot through with oppositions.

Whatever the specific articulation of these they all have the form of the opposition that is the very *arché* of my being, namely, self-other: the form, that is, of some particular concrescence implicated with its own mode of alterity, a center that defines a specific oppugnancy, a particular *here-now* opposing a *there-then*. The articulations may, for example, be myself at this very moment as opposed to myself at an earlier or later moment. It may be the concrescence "I in *my* lifetime" as opposed to "my father in *his*." It may be my weight coming down on my jogging foot and knee as against the asphalt road upon which I run. It may be my attention concentrated upon an intellectual puzzle as opposed to the throbbing pain in my foot. It may be the concrescence I-in-the-room-in-which-I-write, surrounded by all its accoutrements that are part and parcel of my power to focus on the task at hand, as opposed to all that is only on the margins or beyond the range of my attention—the barking dog, the hum of a passing car. It may be my sense of who I am and where I stand in the midst of a colloquy—even if neither of these is articulate or lucidly sensed—as opposed to who others are and where they stand. It may be that sharpest of all senses of opposition that is borne in upon me by the otherness of the other in my most intimate relation. I find that I keep bumping into this other person in a thousand ways, discovering both her limits and mine at the ever-changing frontier where we meet. It may be the intensely concrete perplexity that engages me as opposed to the fugitive resolution that I already know it has. It can be I as opposed to you. It can be any center as opposed to any periphery, any *myself* as over against any *other*. And the range of such possible forms of the appearances of the self-other opposition is virtually infinite. To be the kind of pre-tensive/retrotensive being that I am is precisely to live within the textures of these opposures.

Of course, the most notorious and unforgiving of such opposi-tions in the modern period is that between the subject and the object: the *subject* as mind, consciousness, the mental, as that in which ideas inhere, that at times achieves a kind of ontologically discarnate existence; the *object* that is ontologically distinct from mind, constant, intractable, as mind is not, independent.

Etymology is quite clear on this. The Latin gives us *sub + iacio*, to throw under; *ob + iacio*, to throw against. This radical form of the sub-opposition and of the ob-opposition is in no wise implicated, as such, with the 17th-century mental-entity vs. physical-entity dis-tinction. It rather seems to allude to a kind of bedrock oppugnancy in our nature that can be given a wide range of different articula-tions, as I have observed above. And this leads me to wonder how the paradigmatic opposition of the modern philosophical tradition took shape. Undoubtedly this is connected with the dissemination of the printed page.

Some speculations—and how do we proceed here, since we can have no *written* reports on the nature of an actual oral/aural culture and its sensibility? By ransacking our own residual orality, using a phenomenological and transcendentally deductive analysis.

The oral world has its reality paradigmatically in the spoken, heard, and ritually remembered word—in the ritual action of re-membrance—the world of literacy has its, derives its standard of reality, in the written (eventually printed), read, and physically accumulated and preserved word. Reality in its only important sense for an oral culture is "called" into being by human speech—called "from absence to be on display," as Auden has put it. If this seems an extraordinary—or meaningless—claim, let us not over-look the extent to which this is true even for our contemporary literate selves: how at a given moment the circumambient world of possible appearance is actualized by our acts of speech; how the real—the *focal* and *significant real at a given moment*—is just that that we have by our utterance caused to stand forth from its background; a background that includes the bedrock of our ubiquitous, unreflected, convivially co-present mindbodies, the retrotension of our accreted perceptual experience, the worlds we have "abandoned" and those not yet actualized.

6/21/88

In the midst of our quotidian sayings and doings in what we take to be the ordinary world we never encounter the immutable world embodied in what Merleau-Ponty calls the "constancy hypothesis"—a world behind or beneath the perceptual world believed to be preeminently real and knowable because of this immutability. This reality, depicted in a variety of philosophical styles, answers to the demand laid upon us by the history of philosophy (itself a product of our literacy) in a cluster of images and in the epistemological and ontological values implicated in them. Almost the only bearing that these have upon our ordinary saying and doing, in our moments of literate reflection, is to weaken our ingenuous confidence in the autonomy and ontological value of this quotidian life.

Our ordinary perceptual experience, in striking contrast to the world set forth in the constancy hypothesis, abstracted from this experience, is incessantly changing from morning's first light to twilight's last gleaming, within which, nevertheless, stable worlds are called into being in our human midst, to be replaced, as we "abandon" them, by new stable worlds almost *ad infinitum*. This is the long-familiar way things are; we think nothing of it. *In this context*, the question, "Are these worlds real, did we just conjure them out of thin air?" simply never arises. As we actually live this life there is no room into which this doubt can be intruded. It arises only as we are in thrall to the constancy hypothesis. Only an epistemological analysis in which the values of literacy have been sublimed provides the basis for such an in-principle ecumenic impeachment of the reality of this world.

As the "real world" of our critical, reflected accounts comes more and more to be identified with objects—objects of which the models are printed words within a text—abstracted from their oral/aural provenance, and comes to be thought to be stable and unchanging, static and detached from human speech, so the sense of the evanescence of the realities that are thought to have no more solid ground than human speech and ritual acts of remembrance is taken to be only marginally real or not real at all.

Here in the contrast between orality and literacy we have that characteristic modern articulation of the root opposition in our mindbodily being expressed in the etymological radicals *ob* + *iectum* and *sub* + *iectum*, the opposition, subject vs. object, subjectivity vs. objectivity.

6/22/88

When do we find it necessary, in transacting our business in the ordinary world, to depend upon this comprehensive *philosophical* distinction between the subject and the object, between the cogito and things, bearing with it all of the metaphysical impedimenta of thinking mind and extended body? We do not require it in order to establish that and how knowledge is possible. This does not require establishing. Then is it for the purpose of formulating criteria for evaluating knowledge-claims? But how often is the distinction, subject-object, required for articulating and applying these in particular cases? And in any case, how often in practice are these explicitly formulated? Or do thinking thing and extended thing, subject and object (as these have, on the whole, been used since the 17th century), the cogito and things, our ever-changing consciousness as over against a perduring world, serve rather as tokens in the liturgical reenactment of modern man's exodus from pre-Enlightenment darkness as they mainly do in the orthodox modern liturgy of Descartes' *Discourse on Method*. Does not (prized) objectivity—as compared with (mere) subjectivity—embody modern man's conception of the way he stands (Godlike) in relation to the subject (object) of his knowledge? Yet does this not threaten, at the same time, to reduce him in his so-called subjectivity to a useless passion?

If, as seems likely, this is their principal, if not indeed their sole, function; if, that is, they embody and ritually iterate modern man's conception of his position and power in the universe—and let us not fail to notice that even in this Enlightenment myth it is deeply ambiguous—then their role, by no means on this account lacking in gravity, will have to be differently appraised. From this, of course, it does not follow that in our ordinary doings and sayings we will not find it natural to use for simple description as adverbs and adjectives the words 'subjective', 'objective', and their cognates, unburdened by the weight of their liturgical role. We can quite usefully say, "Poteat exhibited a conspicuous lack of objectivity in his decision," while remaining wholly noncommittal on the subject of the subject-object split in that formulation of it, dear to epistemology since Galileo and Descartes, Locke and Hobbes—where, on the whole, it has done great mischief.

Individuation and socialization are not two different processes, but two faces of the same process. As we do not, strictly, could not, learn the meaning of *I* without, in the same instant, learning the meaning of not-*I*, of *you, they, we;* so our individuation can only proceed simultaneously with our socialization. They emerge together—as the pronouns *I* and *you* and our power to use them emerge—from our as-yet-unreflected mindbodily ground in which the concepts 'individuation' and 'socialization' have as yet no traction and therefore the distinction between individuation and socialization can as yet have none. It is, again, the Cartesian *cogito* that betrays us here. We suppose that reflection begins with the certainty of the *ego* of the *cogito*. But, of course, *tu* is a co-implicate of *ego*, is quite as certain as the latter and equally radical.

6/23/88

I have discovered from etymology more about my *mind* and my *body*—and especially about how they derive from and remain grounded in my *mindbody*—than from any other source. Indeed, etymology has been my principal instrument of research. To follow the history of our language until it disappears into its own prehistory—into the logos implicit in our sentience, motility, and orientation—is to discover that mind is embodied and that the body is enminded; that they are both rooted in the primitive ordinations of our mindbodily energies; that language—our first formal system—has the sinews of our bodies which had them first. It is impossible to study the English word 'tend' in its etymological matrix without being drawn mindbodily, in the most palpable way, into that place where mind and body are one.

6/27/88

"To imagine a language is to imagine a form of life."

Our form of life of course includes the ways that words work among us. The kinds of ways that these can work together *now* is a function of the etymologies whose stamp they still bear with them—bear precisely in the kinds of ways that they naturally behave. Their cognate etymological roots enter into the logic of their behavior, as the way in which the board is laid out for chess enters into the logic of the way different chess pieces behave.

Notice how 'pretend', 'intend', 'retrotend', 'tender' work and you'll (tacitly) know that they have a common root. Knowing how to use a language is in part (tacitly) knowing this. To know this is also to discover the roots of mind, to understand what logos is.

So we don't have to read dictionaries in order to live our form of life. Etymological dictionaries give it historical depth. But it already has that depth in the etymologies of words that we (tacitly) know from our skillful use of them.

Etymology can be the means whereby we (somewhat) lay bare—make explicit—the tacit logos of our mindbodily life. When we discover that the radical meaning of, for example, 'pretend' is "to stretch forth," we begin to see the ways in which the primitive ordinations of our mindbodily energies can simultaneously articulate this word from within themselves and provide the matrix within which we can *introject its meaning*, both in our learning of it and in our subsequent use of it. We can also see how an aid in teaching the meaning of 'pretend' would be to streeeetch oneself forth while saying the word.

And if you ask me how I know this, all I can say is: I have a profound immediate mindbodily sense of it, precipitated by the incorporation of the very words that embody the etymological facts.

Long before we have the anatomist's understanding of the way in which the system of our muscles works in relation to the bones of our skeleton, we have tacitly understood all of this and relied upon our understanding. Knowing the etymology of our language is like this.

6/28/88

When we combine the death of God with the triumph over our imaginations of the view of time as a succession of discrete, atemporal "instants" of (visual) space, we achieve for ourselves the status of "Gods of the fugitive instant," upon whom the "I will be that I will be" of Yahweh is lost; who therefore can no longer understand the self as responsible.

There is nothing—Kant notwithstanding—more bedrock, more

indubitable, better known, with more immediate certitude than the power I have to take responsibility for myself and for the world, insofar as I claim it as my own—if I have not been alienated by abstraction from that ground of all meaning and meaning-discernment, my lively mindbody in the world. Kant performed for modern thought the definitive act of alienation in his first *Critique*. We have to begin by seeing that he got it all wrong—though of course, modern thought was already thoroughly alienated by the time he went to work on it.

7/11/88

Philosophical anthropology, especially since Descartes, has suffered the onus of the subject-object dualism, in theory alternating between the doctrine of man the machine and that of man the useless passion and in practice trying to act simultaneously from both perspectives.

We can shift the axis of this fruitless debate, if we but come to realize that the distinction, subject–object, thinking thing–extended thing, mind–body, does not, Descartes to the contrary notwithstanding, exhaust the forms of "finite substance," for all the power over the natural world in the prodigies of modern natural science and technology that it has afforded; but is, rather, *derived*—from the *truly* radical finite substance, our unreflected convivial mindbodies in their coition with that that is variously and indeterminately over against them. No mean feat. The truth is, the dichotomy thinking thing–extended thing and its variants are *our invention*: heuristically potent but lethal when hypertrophied—modern epistemology's Faustian bargain. In contracting for this promise of mastery, we have forfeited our most archaic power of being by falling under the sway of our own creation.

This saving truth: that reality as it is known in reflection is a reality of our own devising affords a new standpoint from which to investigate human being.

Is this idealism? Certainly not. While it holds that reality as known in reflection is of our own devising, it also holds that the concepts and other usages that issue in reflection and are its instruments arise out of, derive their authority from, and remain grounded in a reality—as intractable as can be—that does not appear in reflection, yet is always manifest at reflection's back, and that continuously asseverates itself in all the quotidian doings and sayings of our unreflected but convivial mindbodies.

Is this, then, neo-Kantian? Again, certainly not. Kant's first *Critique* quite uncritically takes the Cartesian subject-object split as the only ground upon which an authoritative account of how we can have knowledge of objects as such might be formulated. To locate the authority of this dualism *in our own acts of reflection* rather than in the putative bedrock of a given "nature of things," and to disclose the range of options open to us *in* reflection, is to displace the ground of Kant's argument in advance.

Our transition from simple organisms to reflective persons is accomplished as our mindbodies invest themselves in a succession of "figures of their own devising";* as, that is, the logos of our sentience, motility, and orientation issues in a repertoire of increasingly abstract shapings—the ordinations *of* time and space and *in* time and space of our lively and expressive mindbodies: our ordered motility and rhythmical breathing, our song and dance, our patterned, ritual movement in agreement with the cadence of the earth, the civil reenactment of our story, our convivial gestures and speech, the walls of our dwellings and the walls of our city, our sculpture and our painting, and our mathematical projection. Taken together these usages articulate the temporal distensions between no-longer and not-yet, giving therein variant forms to the self-other oppugnancy that is an *arché* of our being in the world. We apprehend the nature of ourselves and of that that is over against us in figures that have themselves been educed from this very opposition. The concepts that are our vectors of the real are themselves derivative of the reality that they bear—so intimate at rock-bottom is the connection between being and knowing.

Usages are what we do and what we say, the repertoire of instruments and gestures that are their means; words that, being habitually used, are usages—*concepts* that can, like the rhapsode's formulaic figure or the dancer's arabesque, draw us mindbodily into a certain mode of being—they are our wonted practices, the tempo and the rhythms of our gait, the pitch and inflections of our voice, the spaces that we traverse to conviviality and the means of doing so, the spaces we will not cross; they are our posture and our bearing—martial or pacific—the pace and style of our speech—clipped or drawling, highly gestural or contained, etc., etc. All these and many other things are usages: we at once *have* them and are *in their midst*.

[* Elizabeth Sewell.]

Ensconced within the actuality of life amid these usages, we do not ask the question, What, here, is mental and what physical? 'Mental' and 'physical' are not notions that can have a purchase amid these first-order doings. They are derivative of a second-order reflective activity and arise only in obedience to a particular—and narrow—form of curiosity that just happens to have been the paradigmatic one since Descartes made his famous announcement about finite substances.

Speaking and hearing speech are things we do all the day long without ever wondering whether these are mental or physical or partly mental and partly physical things that we are doing. The sense that in this we stand on autonomous bedrock is violated by the thinking thing–extended thing option that we are given by modernity. My speaking and your hearing are, in the event, commonplace phenomena to which this distinction has no application. Speaking is *speaking*: I say words aloud to you and you understand; I actualize a potentiality of my lively mindbody—like walking or pointing or singing a tune—and you in hearing actualize a potentiality in turn. But because we can and do analyze the physiology of speech and hearing we are seduced into the supposition that the something extra, over and above the physiology—namely, *meaning* the words and *interpreting* the meaning—must be something mental and begin to wonder how ever we can get these two sorts of entity together. But we already *have* speaking and hearing as autonomous bedrock. 'Mental' and 'physical' are derivative of and parasitical upon this "figure of our own devising," without authority in themselves; only what we impute to them, which now we must reclaim as what they are.

7/18/88

One doesn't (physically) *speak* the words and then on the side or in addition (mentally) *mean* them. Speaking our words and meaning them are one and the same thing. She says: "You *say* you love me, but you don't really mean it." One can make perfectly good (even philosophical) sense of this remark without invoking a distinction between saying and meaning; *certainly* without trading upon the (physically) saying and (mentally) meaning distinction.

Saying "I love you"—saying anything at all—has a context: on one hand, the fine grain of intonation, affect, gestures (body language); on the other, the coarse grain of steadfastness.

The context in which this woman's lover utters the words, "I love you," is such that it gives the lie to the words: he looks at his watch; he philanders. He doesn't—he can't—mean them in the only sense that matters to his "beloved," not because, though having (physically) spoken the words, he has—deliberately or inadvertently— refrained from (mentally) meaning them.

Mind and matter, meaning and its incarnation, are at bottom inseparable, for they are consanguine creatures of the figuring powers of our mindbodies

The very usages that arise in our mindbodily coition with the world themselves define the form of that coition of which they are the offspring.

The whole of what we call our mental life has to be reimagined in the light of this. It is impossible for us to dwell in our own acts of speech as words directed in good faith to another person and, at the same time, abscond from our integral incarnate selves by invoking the dualism thinking thing–extended thing. Erstwhile Cartesians will find here definitive healing of this dualism.

7/19/88

Meaning comes to be borne by and can make its appearance in the world through the most utterly ordinary of corporeal vectors; but of course never apart from *some* such—in words, gestures, musical themes, rhythms, visual and auditory motifs, dance, mime, poetic figures, metaphors, etc., etc. Iterated, they become usage. All these cases of course (and many others as well) are the issue of human intention, though we must steadfastly resist our culturally induced impulse to depict this as having an intention to mean a given thing that then cathects some token that will serve as its vector. Here are not three entities, but one. Of course, natural events and phenomena can also be such vehicles.

A word, a gesture, a musical signature, for example, and their use, when iterated amid our ordinary doings and sayings, are all usages—both the fine and the coarse fabric of our convivial life is a sum of usages. Indeed, from one point of view, the whole texture of our life is a function of these—application to which of the epithets "mental thing," "physical thing" would be absurd, inasmuch as they constitutionally endue our mindbodily life with its form and style.

To *be* a concept is to be a vector that has a wonted use, is employed by users; for one to *have* a concept is to be able to call upon a usage, recognize its appropriateness in context; doing this is nothing less than knowing where—in the world—you are.

The most potent instrument of human control over our environment is the word, the instrument of reflection and hence of all explicit knowledge—which we have taken to be the paradigm of all knowledge as such. Both Greeks and Hebrews saw 'word' as imbued with peculiar power; indeed, as the very embodiment of the real.

In modernity with its in-principle ecumenic doubt, whereby all significant knowledge can only be the outcome of a skeptical inquiry, the evaluation of explicit, that is, verbally reflected, knowledge suffered hypertrophy, causing a further devaluation of the tacit knowledge which gives form to our ordinary doings and sayings, and which is in fact the *conditio sine qua non* of all explicit knowledge.

In such a setting, it was natural that *concepts*, in other words, verbal usages by which we classify particular things, should be taken to have an intimate, perhaps exclusive, affiliation with *words*, with, in other words, the general instruments of our reflective, that is, our *mental* (as opposed to our physical or full mindbodily), life. In short, in this view words and concepts come, in our imaginations, to have this intimate logical bond with one another and with the *mental* (as opposed to physical and mindbodily).

In this view, to be a concept is to be a word-like mental entity; for one to have a concept is to apprehend such an entity in one's "mind."

Yet, as we have seen, meaning appears in tokens from which it is inseparable; and grasping this meaning is achieved by the full, integral mindbodily appropriation of the constellations that these tokens form in the setting of our other usages.

If we reject the imperial claims of the mind-body dualism that extends over even the remotest outposts of our imaginations, in favor of the integral mindbody as the ultimate ground of all meaning and meaning-discernment, we will be struck by the analogies between word-concepts, as they have hitherto been understood, and other usages that are embedded in and serve our quotidian life, undistorted by intimations of some "mental"-like–"physical"-like opposition.

This will enhance the possibility that we can ingenuously accept the authority of our common sense that dualism has impeached;

and will endorse the reality and convey the authentic feel of our unreflected mindbodily life.

What would it be like to think of word-concepts as, in important ways, resembling all other usages in our life? Are not the following—to take them as examples—strikingly analogous to word-concepts; indeed may it not be philosophically illuminating to call them "concepts" under certain circumstances?—an habituated gesture, say, a salute, a beckoning finger, even a sidelong glance—do not their applications assist us in defining and recognizing a situation in the way that we have assumed that word-concepts uniquely do? None of these is spoken aloud in the way that word-concepts often are. Yet do they not "speak," these wonted gestures—giving form and identity to the world? And what of a familiar musical interval, say C E G C, or the key signature, D minor, and its many musical possibilities. Mayn't these lead us, as a spoken word-concept often does, to recognize, "name," and appraise our situation in the world in a certain way rather than in some other. Or, finally, take the case of the visual motifs—the common import for our upright bodies of the vertical or the diagonal line in sculpture, painting, and architecture. Do these not, without addressing merely "mental-like" or spoken concepts, serve as well as they to establish us in the world?

7/20/88

An extensive catalogue of similar cases would be boring beyond endurance and would shed little further light on these matters. The essential truth is simple: concepts are usages, words that have a wonted use among us; and like all other usages, the meaning that they bear is not apprehended by the "mind" (as opposed to the body), but rather in the integral mindbody's eros for all meaning. An appeal to a "thinking thing" sheds no light, while sowing much confusion.

The constancy that the changeful world of our commonsense experience exhibits at a given moment derives from the stable forms of the mindbody's own integrity as sentient, motile, and oriented; from the precipitate of past experience, husbanded in its usages; and from the world-forming powers of our convivial gestures and speech.

Nothing I do is a discrete, brute occurrence, unenformed by a meaning and telos, ranging from the concrete, mute axioms of significance that shape my sentience and orientation, on one hand, to the historical drama within in which I see myself as acting, on the other, with of course a rich hierarchy of possibilities in between.

We can usefully distinguish between the logos that, unreflected, enforms our quotidian doings and sayings and our reflected second-order descriptions (explanations, justifications) of these. Of course, even these latter are not all of the same order, do not have the same range of logical efficacy, the same bearing upon, efficacy for, the same role to perform in, the elucidation of these doings and sayings.

7/21/88

It is an epitome of our Enlightenment conceit that intellection is tacitly taken, in the subtlest of ways, to be a discarnate transaction among crystalline ideas, uncontaminated by any gross affiliation with our carnal being. For us, therefore, the very paradigm of the barely literate dolt is someone who "moves his lips when he reads." Yet, reading silently is a recently cultivated ideal and skill. Until Enlightenment literacy forced this repression upon us, insisting by implication that silent reading from the printed page should be a strictly atemporal intellectual intuition of eternal meanings borne by their static vectors, it was obvious that the apprehension of words ingenuously involved their being *said*—by their *incorporation* in the act of being spoken aloud or at least by the silent moving of our carnal lips, tongue, and glottis.

We cannot take possession of words by our "pure" intellect, since, quite simply, there is no such thing. We apprehend them through our integral mindbodies; and "moving our lips as we read" is a mark of this fact. Why would this ever happen, if it were not a condition of the comprehension of a text?

The distinction between the sensible species and the intelligible species by means of which we could once talk about the difference between the *physical* word—whether written and seen or spoken and heard—and its *intelligible* meaning is now imprecise at best and, in any case, of dubious value. It presupposes a dualism, thought to be bedrock rather than derivative, that goes back at least as far as Plato, and that is here under attack.

I say these things not in the belief that, once said, they are likely to be hotly contested. I say them rather because they exert their power over our imaginations as things this culture believes go without saying and therefore, until they are said, it embraces uncritically.

7/26/88

Earlier I have written that the Enlightenment insisted by implication "that silent reading from the printed page should be a strictly atemporal intellectual intuition of eternal meanings borne by their static vectors"—an observation that, though rather infelicitously delivered, is of interest here as a further mark of dualism: thought, our comprehension of thought-things, does not, in this view, require the mediation of our carnality.

I think that Descartes is one of the very few ever expressly to have uttered this patent absurdity [*Discourse*, pt. IV]—though it would be foolish to underestimate the potency and ubiquity among us of its spiritual seductiveness. If this is so, the question becomes: why, then, Poteat, do you utter it here?

The answer is not a simple one because it cuts to the very heart of what and how we believe what we believe—how we uphold our believings; what we value and how we do so.

The Enlightenment is not only what it is able and consents, under the pressure of the official theory, explicitly to say about itself. It is fundamentally a fund of covert intentions, notices, and intimations that issue in images and values rarely recognized in themselves and even more rarely spoken of. It is the explicit "official" self-definition that carries the weight and obscures the radical truth. The world as apprehended is not solely a creature of explicit articulation. Its shaping in our reflection has already been well begun behind our backs.

These "images" and "values"—I place these in scare-quotes in order to indicate that I do not use these words as they would be used in ordinary discourse, or even as they might be used in discussions of art and culture, or as in philosophical remarks upon the nature of imagination or upon axiology; they refer rather to the *most primitive* meaning-giving, coherence-seeking forms that are generated in our mindbodily intercourse with the world, beyond the reach of articulation, but yet "showing" themselves—these "images" and "values" that are ascendant in our imaginations long before they are recognized as such, but are always at our backs, issuing through articulation in our more or less lucent notions and explicit appraisals, are the dynamic mindbodily source of our feats of meaning-discernment.

Words therefore that appear plainly absurd when read as the direct language of everyday, may, when read as an indirect language, disclose the most potent because covert images and values of our imaginations.

"Our thought, our comprehension of thought things, does not, in this view, require the mediation of our carnality": in roundly uttering these words that I know to be absurd on their face, I am doing nothing other than allowing myself to give *explicit* expression to images and values whose *tacit* pressure I, as a denizen of this deeply dualistic culture, incessantly feel and have vigilantly to resist.

7/28/88

At what interface between ourselves and the cultural world of our own devising do these buried "images" and "values" arise; at what meeting between our most archaic mindbodily intentions and the artifacts—both "conceptual" and "material"—that, obeying these intentions, we fashion, as rejoinder, the images and values that in our ordinary affairs we rely upon and often even openly profess?

Obviously, different such junctures give rise to different repertoires of images and values. The question then has to be addressed on a case-by-case basis.

Here what concerns us is the divorce between our thought and our carnality; between meaning and the "corporeal" tokens that are taken to be its vectors; between the "physical" speaking of words and the meaning of them; between thinking thing and extended thing, mind and body, subject and object.

To raise this question is of course not at all to imply that such distinctions have never or could never serve a practical or philosophical purpose, on the contrary; rather it is to suggest that they are after all not *heteronomies* to which we are subject but rather are the contingent outcome of our convivial mindbodily nisus toward meaning, coherence, and value, that answer to specific intentions. The dualism that is here under attack was after all midwife to science and technology. To claim this however is not to claim that it is the necessary form of *all* thought and therefore the setting of all philosophical anthropology. It comes to saying: the meaning (and value) of the subject-object distinction is its usefulness in a language.

8/9/88

In the present case it is our movement about in the environment of literacy that has at once evoked from and vested in our imaginations these images and values. This is a world of uniform printed letters uniformly spaced, forming words in uniform rows, clearly opposed to the surfaces upon which they are inscribed in visual space.

Contrast this image and this value with those of orality where words do not stand out clearly against a background that is spatial, static, and lucent, but are likely to be entangled in a plexus where several different layers of discourse converge in time, different levels of sound, different degrees of dialectical intensity; and whose background is the dynamic and relentless forward surge of the time of lively speech. No denizen of an oral culture, even were he inclined and able to entertain an ecumenic view of his own practice, is likely, as was Descartes—that creature of print culture par excellence—to make the "clear and distinct" the paradigm of an intuitively irresistible idea.

Thus inscribed in visual space, words are recoverable in a manner that spoken words are not. Time as the mere temporal dimension of static objects in space tends, in our imaginations, to be assimilated to these objects in their (visual) spatiality and therefore itself to become "space-like." Then, as this picture has it, its "eternal," atemporal "moments" have become as replicable as the abstract eternal and atemporal magnitudes of (visual) space—which invites the construction that any exactly *replicable* moment (word) is the *same* moment, even as a given *printed* word in its spatial position on a page continues in each successive moment of its duration to be an exact replica of itself, according to this view. I can more or less exactly return to the previously read word as I cannot exactly do so in the same way with the previously heard.

8/10/88

These contrasting images and values, of course, give rise to the implicit distinction—as old as philosophy itself—between the dynamic, evanescent world of the oral/aural—evanescent as it seems from the point of view of literacy—and the static, permanent world of literacy. The relation of the subject to the object, in such a scheme, is the analogue of the relation of the reader to a text and of God to the world.

Our tuition at the hands of literacy taught us that that is intelligible which, like written and printed words (logoi), is static, permanent, therefore recoverable (in the manner that a printed word is recoverable).

Obviously oral/aural people have words and obviously in their own usages they recognize that words, by definition, have a measure of permanence. Their meanings are not altered in mid-conversation.

Until printing (writing), however, the image of words as enjoying an exemption from the temporal surge of oral/aural life could not take shape and eventually usurp all authority in the imagination. The time of the endurance of printed words is *bound* time—confined within the limits of a finite, fully recoverable "eternal" text.

The *mind* in this scheme therefore tends to be thought of as only truly itself when it is *rational*, when, that is to say, it is freed of all those inherently irrational, that is, "unlimited," infinite, temporal, protean elements of subjectivity such as characterize the moil and ruck of our convivial, oral/aural, mindbodily life, by its concentration upon the fixed, limited *therefore* rational, *viz.*, the (written) word. The cultivation and subliming of these real powers of mind for grasping fixed relations—paradigmatically in geometry, arithmetic, and formal logic—inevitably resulted in the tacit denigration of all our other powers of judgment and discrimination. We do not cease to rely upon the logos that enforms our sentience, motility, orientation, perception, and practice. It only loses any standing as logos in our accounts of our feats of coming to know; and therefore plays at best a merely minor role in our general views of the nature of humankind.

Freed from these putatively irrational elements of "subjectivity"—what Plato designated *thumos* and *epithumia*, in contrast to *nous*—the mind can realize itself in the contemplation of what in this picture is represented as being *true* because *eternal*, as written words are "eternal" in contrast to spoken ones: namely, Plato's *eidos*; Descartes' "clear and distinct ideas"; the eternal because mathematically expressible primary qualities of things—in contrast to the "infinity" of the changeful world of secondary qualities, etc., etc.

In the philosophical environment in which these images and values are superordinate, only that can count as knowledge—as opposed to mere *doxa*—that is the outcome of a skeptically induced inquiry, issuing in analysis and explicitation. Of course, *in fact*, only a very small fraction of what we know and rely upon as being known—even if this does not stand with us as "what we know"—meets or has ever met this test.

8/16/88

As rationality has been depicted as the exact noetic complement to essentially static and "eternal" forms, concepts, and mathematical relations, themselves the analogues of written or printed words, so consciousness has been pictured as having a lucent center that shades off into a darkening penumbra of the exotic, suspect, epistemologically problematic or irrelevant. It is not of course that, under this regime, consciousness has not been recognized as having complexity and depth. It is rather that its putatively lucent center has been the perspective from which the nature and meaning of that complexity and depth have been construed. Think of how the human wit embodied in ancient languages, fable, history, poesy, mathematics, morals, theology, philosophy, and (even) science, all abandoned by Descartes, is disesteemed when viewed from the perspective of the clarity and distinctness of the *cogito*.

There are perils in my using consciousness here. Its affiliations with the whole repertoire of usages in the psychological and epistemological discourse of the tradition will trigger retroversions into it.

Consciousness is however not a "faculty" defined by a lucent center that has been sublimed. It is not a "faculty" at all. Nor can we say that it is a power that interpenetrates our mindbodily life, as if there were, on the one side, our mindbodily life and, on the other, this power which interpenetrates it, as for the anatomist, oxygen interpenetrates our bodies—wherein a body is conceivable that is not so interpenetrated. Consciousness, in other words, does not have a *relationship* to my mindbody. It is, rather, one of its existential modalities. Our investigation of this therefore must keep in view the ubiquitous asseveration in all our doings of the convivial, as-yet-undifferentiated mindbody as the radix of the world of our reflection. This mindbody is the radical given; all else is derivative of it.

Consciousness, then, is the *whole of our mindbodily life* viewed from the standpoint of its power to appreciate meaning, from our tropisms toward light, warmth, equilibrium—physical and existential—to the style of a gesture, the intention of a musical motif, the configuration of events in time, the appositeness of a word, the propriety of an act, an expression of a human face, the law of non-contradiction and excluded middle, the force of the question, Why is there something rather than nothing?—even as we see, looked at from a slightly different angle, that a logos permeates every stratum and unifies all strata of our mindbodily life: our sentience, motility, and orientation; the expressive life of speech, gesture, song and dance; our dreams and fantasies; quite as much as a logos—the same logos, in emerging articulation—enforms our tacit powers of judging and the "intellectual" life expressed in the explicit formulation and solution of practical and theoretical problems, and the projection of a general theory of the nature of things.

8/17/88

Thinking thing and extended thing—and all the other dualisms—mind/body, the mental/the physical, subject/object; cognates all, but by no means interchangeable usages—are abstractions from the dynamic actuality of our noetic coition with the world, subsidized by literacy's static paradigm of the knowable and the "atemporal" rational powers that putatively alone bear upon it. These are the progeny of literacy.

And this tendency to imagine that these abstractions "describe" our knowings is nurtured by the belief that only that can count as being knowledge that is the outcome of analysis and explicitation, issuing from a skeptically induced systematic inquiry. Usually, perhaps always, the only relation that such an explicit description can have to our actual feats of knowing is after the fact, which is to say only when it is prescinded from their dynamic actuality, possibly serving some celebratory function. Of course, these images, values, and beliefs have been deeply introjected into the sensibility of every denizen of this culture and have their so-potent logical efficacy in the practice of our knowings precisely in being only tacitly exerted.

Thus literacy abstracts: it abstracts the word from its lively use; usages are transmogrified into "mental" (as opposed to physical) entities; into concepts—*universalis in intellectu*, in the language of the old debate—modeled upon the written word that, unlike the spoken, is static and "atemporal" before the discarnate mind.

8/19/88

Once the "mental" has been solidly established over against the "physical," "thinking thing" over against "extended thing," it seems inevitable that these distinctions should be, as it were, driven "inward." Thought will come to be distinguished from its "outward" and audible sign, as the words I write down to express my thought come to be distinguished from and are taken to be only "contingently" related to my "inner" mental activity of thinking them; and as the sign that I write down comes to be perceived as having an entirely factitious relation to its semantic object in the world.

This mentalistic dementia reaches its perfection in Husserl's pure transcendental ego, from which the only deliverance is a complete change of venue. About *this* Jacques Derrida is right. His radicalism however is in the end, or rather at the beginning, aborted, for he does not shift the radix of the debate. He only turns it 180° on the axis of "presence," yielding "absence"—a disenchanted child of literacy whose own residual orality is concealed from him by the afterimage of "presence."

One will not however conclude from a close observation of our actual speech acts that the relation between the signifier and the signified is arbitrary, contingent, or factitious. On the contrary. To be sure, there are, in their course, the elements often coming to pass in time—the "contingency" that is inherent in temporal flow; in short, *happenings*. There is, too, the sense of the indeterminacies attendant upon our groping toward the perfectly apposite word. But "groping" is a reaching out for a "something in particular," even if at the outset we do not yet know "what exactly in particular"; and "apposite" means "fitness," fitness to a linguistic state of affairs already anticipated because nebulously taking shape.

Speaking is a seamless, dynamic intentional act; in every case, however routine, an actualization of the mindbody's plenary powers. If you doubt this, closely scrutinize the participants in a lively colloquy. It makes no better sense to apply the either/or of necessary/contingent to the relation between the signifier and the signified or that between thought and its vectors (even if we could intelligibly draw such a distinction in the case of the latter) than it does to wonder whether, as I run, the relation between my feet and the places on the ground where they strike is necessary or contingent. In the world as I directly experience it in my act of running, the question is without meaning. We talk this way about the relation between the signifier and the signified only when we have absconded from the actualities of lively speech.

By contrast, if we focus upon our acts of writing, new possibilities appear. The act of writing is like lively speech in that those same contingencies and the same sense of indeterminacies that attend a speech-event, dynamically unfolding in time, are also present in the act of composing/writing. The activity of putting our thoughts on paper is dynamic. But so soon as this act is complete, a dynamic activity with its intentional flow comes to rest in a static *terminus ad quem*: the written word. From being a writer, until this moment still dwelling in my own orality, I am forthwith transformed into a *reader*, even if only of my own static, written-down words. In this instant, if but for an instant, I become a creature of literacy, imbibing its images, values—and questions. It is now that I am likely, my focus shifted, to raise the question, Is the relation between the signifier and the signified necessary or contingent—and, if either, then in what sense? When we embark upon this course, we soon come seriously to misrepresent the nature of our fundamental relation to the world.

8/23/88

How then are we, from the perspective of these *Investigations*, to run the gauntlet between subjectivism and objectivism as we attempt to think in a new way about memory and hope?

As we have seen, my mindbodily life is, from one point of view, just the fabric of its pretensions and retrotensions. Because of these *pretensions* there is a *not-yet* that is nevertheless contemporaneous with *now*; and because of these *retrotensions* there is a *no-longer* that is similarly contemporaneous with *now*.

If my mindbody lacked this (pre)*tensive* and (retro)*tensive* character, a musical motif would fall upon deaf ears. To hear three musical notes as a melody, the second note must at once pre*tend* the third and retro*tend* the first. By the same token, if it lacked this *pre*(tensive) and *retro*(tensive) character, I should hear all "three notes" at once; in other words, I should hear them as a chord. [Indeed, without these pretensions and retrotensions I should not be able to grasp the meaning of 'pretension' and 'retrotension'.] There must be—therefore there is—this kind of mindbodily matrix as ground for my dwelling in and apprehending this musical figure. All hope and all memory are made possible by this pretension and retrotension; which is to say *human* existence as such is thus made possible.

This is of course the way in which I most immediately apprehend the temporality of my mindbodily existence in the world. When in reflection I abstract myself—especially when this reflection takes place in a theater of reflection dominated by images and values drawn from the visible linearity of printed words upon a page—the past is likely to be depicted as *absent*, radically "out of sight," "unreturnable"; to be "out of mind" as the printed words I have finished reading are absent, since "out of sight." In this view the *present* recedes into the past just as the words in a line of type recede from sight as I read, moving my eyes from left to right. By the same token, the *future*, in this theater of reflection, is equally *absent*, because equally "out of sight," as are the words on the printed page to which my eyes have yet to come.

Of course, my tonic mindbody, in every present moment both pretending the future and retrotending the past, is, for me, inextricably implicated with the world and its unidirectional, irreversible flow. Even so, neither the logical distinctness nor the existential reality of memory and hope are compromised by the fact that I also grow irreversibly older. [Such a remark tempts me, child of Enlightenment and literacy that I am, to think: growing old is a "natural," i.e., objective, phenomenon; memory and hope are merely subjective. So to construe the matter is of course to surrender ground already taken in these *Investigations*.]

If I talk about the "shattering of the past" and its "unreturnability," I conflate the fact, on one hand, of the irreversible flow of the world in which we find ourselves embrangled with, on the other, the retrotensions and pretensions within the web of which we apprehend this flow and upon which our memory and hope are grounded. For reflection the irreversibility of the flow of the world and the pretensive/retrotensive form of my mindbodily life in its midst are of two *logically* heterogeneous orders. In existence nevertheless they cohere, since they are equally grounded in my mindbodily life in the world. The distinction between the subjective and the objective has no *work* to do here; only much *mischief*.

All this of course means that memory and hope are inextricably implicated with the usages and artifacts of my convivial mindbodily life in the midst of the cultural and natural world—even, indeed, in the repertoire of the motor skills of my muscles, incorporated and sustained within my history; in which, no less, memory and hope are husbanded. [Yes, I *am* saying that memory is as well preserved in and hope as well issues from the particular pretensions and retrotensions of the muscular skills that have in my life borne and adapted to the impact of the world.] Wherever the pretensive and retrotensive structure of our mindbodily life is present therein are memory and hope embedded. When therefore attrition is wrought upon these usages, artifacts, and skills, memory will fade and hope will die.

Acting on the authority of X is one thing; identifying, articulating, and justifying X as authority is something else. This is doubly so where X is not an authority that we are given to *articulating* and *invoking* as we act upon it, but rather is just a practice: what we do, what we are given to doing. To attend *explicitly* to that upon whose authority we have, in acting, unreflectingly relied entails the application to it in reflection of a repertoire of concepts. This repertoire explicitly formulated and applied to what was, in our acting, tacit, may well be grossly—or finely—incoherent with the actual tacit "logical" bonds that form the fabric, structure, and telos of what we do *on this occasion*, what we are given to doing: bonds of believings and beliefs; attitudes, evaluations, and their bonds sedimented as values, myths, fantasies, images, the metaphorical intentionalities of our language; our styles and rhythms of speech and movement, our repertoire of gestures; our manners, diction, intonation, and convivial affects; all overdetermined and complexly interacting dynamically with one another. All these and more form the context, establish the logos, of what we do. They also are the form and mode of our mindbodily dwelling in the world.

When we perform this second-order activity of "defining, articulating, and justifying X as authority," the probability is very great that we will acritically rely upon the conceptual repertoire of the Enlightenment epistemological tradition that is in our bones. If we do, we will systematically misconstrue what it means to "act on the authority of X," when X is something upon which we *tacitly* depend because it is first and foremost embodied in what we are *given to doing*. For this tradition is conceptually inhibited from making the distinction between acting upon the authority embodied in what we are given to doing and acting upon authority that has been made explicit. This ever-present possibility of misconstrual is the reason we can't take at face value what someone says about why and how she does what she does. She may be a very bad judge of this because she brings the wrong set of concepts to the interpretation of acts. Of course, we can always agree that this is what she *says* she does and consider whether doing what she says is good or bad, right or wrong. Then we would at least be clear as to what *we* are doing; and there would be a kind of intellectually satisfying density in our analysis, more there than meets the eye.

Consider this. Vickie Hearne says:* "One way of explaining how Winkler (a brilliant trainer of horses) was able to succeed with Halla (a horse thought by most trainers to be 'crazy') is to say that he had a better story to tell himself and her about the nature of horsemanship and horses than riders who failed with her did. He had to have had, for one thing, a story about how what appears to be horse insanity may be—even must be, most of the time—evidence of how powerful equine genius is, and how powerfully it can object to incoherence, and he must have had a story like that about Halla which would move him to keep thinking and trying when things got rough. . . . The stories we tell matter, and not only do stories reclaim the beauty of crazy horses but also stories lead to insanity in the first place."

When my horse and I go through the figures of dressage, relying upon the integrity of our bodies, upon the integrity, too, of the cultivated but now subordinate intimate bond between our bodies, upon the hours of accepting and embodying a discipline, subject to the telos of achieving a more harmonious relation to ourselves, to one another, and to our mutual being in the world, we are acting upon the *authority* of our bodies, the bond between us and our discipline.

In writing these words I am describing the *authority* upon which in doing so I rely—describing it in the way that a horseman would, telling the right story about my horse and myself: "This is what's going on here," I should be saying.

Suppose however I describe "what's going on here" in the way a philosopher would who in principle shies at any "anthropomorphic" suggestion of horses "powerfully objecting to incoherence," or in the way of a neobehaviorist psychologist. These accounts would certainly be logically incoherent with the former. But, more important, if the philosopher or psychologist were to take up dressage, this incoherence might seriously impede the achievement of this equestrian *praxis*. Indeed, it might, as Hearne suggests, actually lead to equine [and even possibly to] equestrian insanity.

9/17/88

A thesis of *Polanyian Meditations* is that our feats of reflection and intellection—the exercise of our so-called higher powers—are rooted

[* *Adam's Task.*]

in and derivative of our most primitive forms of sentience, motility, and orientation; that our "minds" are inextricably implicated with our "bodies"; that our visible gestures and audible speech are connate with the meaning and integrity of our mindbodily existence; that the motifs of our speaking are consanguine with those of our movement. In saying this I am relying upon my radix in the world that everywhere and relentlessly asseverates itself within the web of my ordinary ways of being, upon which, of course, both the philosophic tradition of the West and Western science are parasitical and to which we would move quite directly, asking no one's leave, but for the grave insult inflicted by the Cartesian Enlightenment upon our natural trust in common sense. I have tried to gain for my reader this basal shift in sensibility not by a count-by-count impeachment of that which prevails in modernity—a task which in any case is impossible—but rather by dwelling in it myself as fully and with as much pathos as possible and to report from within it, with many different rhetorical stratagems, upon the different rhythms and motifs of our human situation in the world.

If however this claim is to carry conviction, I must not only assert it and adduce arguments in support of it; the very tonus and torque of my language must, as I write, themselves embody and express the reflexive relationship between my words and the tonus and torque of my existentially actual mindbody. The pretension by my mindbody of its own written or spoken words and the simultaneous retrotension by my written or spoken words of their mindbodily source is a bedrock fact which must be allowed to appear in the text.

What was the method I was practicing in writing the book such that I came to notice this relation between my mindbody and the language issuing from it, in spite of the pressure upon me in this culture to fail to do so? Succinctly put, the answer is: I paid attention at once and equally to *what* I was trying to say, to the *way* I found myself saying it, and to the *import* of the way I found myself saying it *from within the picture I had of myself*—the picture, namely, of a dynamic, sentient, motile, oriented maker with language and gesture, a wordsmith, a poet through and to whose expressively versatile mindbody a world appears. And while I was doing *this* I attended also to what *I*, my mindbody, in the *midst* of it all, was doing.

Let us look at a case. I find myself writing the words "the as-yet-unreflected is opaque to reflection." Obviously this is itself a reflected reference to "the reflected" and "the as-yet-unreflected." But

I am not merely *juxtaposing* the words in my sentence; I am by means of them reporting as one who is caught up mindbodily *in* the world upon a state of affairs of which I claim to *know*. Or, more accurately, in writing these words, I am making *reflectively* present to myself something that in virtue of this very reflection I now know and can say I know. Yet, in order for me to know of the "as-yet-unreflected" and the "reflected," and to know, too, that the former is opaque to the latter—which fact I come to know *as I am writing the sentence*, the writing at once *bringing forth* what I know and *asserting* what I know—there must be some sense in which I *already "know"* the as-yet-unreflected and its relation to the reflected; know an indeterminate "something or other" that is resistant to reflection while being continuous with it. If this is the case, can it then be true that the as-yet-unreflected is *opaque* to reflection? If it were *entirely* opaque could I grasp, either in reflection or in any other way, the relationship between reflection and that which is and is "known" to be opaquely beyond it? Is it not, indeed, because both reflection and that which are its opaque antecedents—my motility, sentience, orientation, and the gestural antecessors and complements of speech—*are tacitly known in my mindbodily tonicity itself*? My mindbodily being as the ubiquitous ground of all meaning and meaning-discernment, through the whole range and hierarchy of its modalities, tonically comprehends all these. If this were not so, would I be inclined as I am, quite ingenuously, to write the sentence, "The as-yet-unreflected is opaque to reflection"?

Now, if my mindbodily tonicity is radical, a datum by which I am immediately, comprehensively, and ubiquitously confronted within the most ordinary activities of being alive in the world, then every expression of its being from simple orientation, to speaking, to the drawing of inferences within a logical calculus is enformed by a logos directed toward order, meaning, rationality, and value. If I wish then to discover these, to cause to stand forth in the reflective acts of writing and speaking the truth possessed by my mindbody in the world—from the opacity to reflection of the as-yet-unreflected to the products of mathematical heuristics, with gesture and speech in between—I must attend to the multifarious expressions of them in the entire range of my mindbody's modes of being.

In such a view, of course, my language will come to be seen as continuous with gesture, as gesture is continuous with sentience and orientation. If this is the case, if my language is, even if singularly powerful, but *one* of the modes of my mindbody's expressions, and is analogous to and consanguine with them all, then its grammar, syntax, meaning, semantic and metaphorical intentionality are portended in the grammar, syntax, meaning, and semantic intentionality of my mindbody. Language itself—its grammar, syntax, and especially its etymology—will be seen to embody in its own formal properties the order, meaning, rationality, and value that it derives from the mindbody's own primitive ordinations, and that it retrotends.

If I pay attention then to what I write and say, alert to this ontological bond among the modes of my mindbodily expressions of order, meaning, rationality, and value, then I shall discover *in the very language I find myself using* both the unity of "body" and "mind" before the distinction has arisen and the things I most deeply know and value. Far from this being a surprising discovery, even less a controversial one, it is rather what we recognize could not be otherwise, once the Cartesian scales have fallen from our eyes.

Earlier I said that as I write (or speak) a sentence I am both *bringing forth* what I know and *asserting* it. It is quite clear that speech understood to be doing the one is different from speech understood to be doing the other, though no description of it which does not take these both into account is complete.

In my writing and speaking I make a world appear. I am more likely to see that this is so, if what I write or speak issues from an effort to formulate a novel or even just a difficult thought; but it is no less the case that the sentence 'snow is white' is true if and only if "snow is white" makes a world appear, brings forth for me what I know.

The writing or speaking of the words that bring forth for me the world that I then know also makes a public announcement of this; these are the acts in which I *assert* what I know.

Philosophic interest in the words we say and write has centered almost exclusively upon the way in which they *assert*, hardly at all upon the multitude of ways they *make a world appear*. Therefore, logical form and assertability conditions have been its preoccupations. Usually the kinds of paradigms around which the discussion has turned—"the cat is on the mat," "the present King of France is bald," and the like—however well they may have served to reflect upon what we say and write, regarded as *assertions*, have been trivial to the point of invisibility as models of the ways in which what we say and write brings forth for ourselves what we know, and makes a world appear. Small wonder therefore that the philosophic tradition has failed to notice that language itself, its grammar, syntax, and especially its etymology, is pregnant with order, meaning, rationality, and value; and that it retrotends these in its own pre-lingual substance.

9/21/88

In *Polanyian Meditations* I am, *inter alia*, trying to make explicit the "conceptual commitments" which I find implicated in the ordinary, unreflected practice of my incarnate existence. There are many impediments to my doing this. According to the explicit conceptual commitments of the Enlightenment culture of which I am a creature, including of course its commitments as to what constitutes the licit uses of the concept 'conceptual commitment', the suggestion above that there are such embodied in my unreflected practice will sound strange. Moreover, as I undertake to discover these unreflected "believings" of mine, the only instruments of reflection at my disposal are those of the unreconstructed conceptual repertoire of the discourse of the Enlightenment. This is an omnipresent seduction. Therefore I have systematically to revise this discourse, lest the very language I use tacitly conceal the reality and logical import of these commitments.

This then means that I must formulate and grasp my argument for myself and *at the same time* revise conceptually the very language which is the argument's medium. Without this simultaneous revision these mindbodily commitments of mine cannot be made both to stand out in themselves against the background of the discourse of the philosophic tradition and to be perceived as having specific logical and epistemological imports. I must not only discover and then acknowledge in a reflection upon reflection that I *have* these commitments; I must also actively appropriate them as the marks of my *actual situation* in the world and as the *concrete motives* of my being as I think and speak of myself, to which, *bona fides* requires me to admit, I have no alternative. I must be able to say, *Here I am*, recognizing that in fact this is an alternative way of saying, *this I believe*, indeed, this I cannot *but* believe. My mindbody in the world is axiologically determined*—that is, through and through ingenuously disposed toward value.

When I have thus formulated my argument I have then to address it to you in what at the outset is recognizably our mutual native language, carefully revising it as I go, however, in order to

[* Robert E. Cushman.]

make it less and less recognizable, hoping thereby to make the "obvious" fact of the existence of these commitments less unfamiliar than they are in the unreconstructed discourse of the Enlightenment. This very procedure is the one I undertook for myself as I groped for the language that would bring forth what I know.

All this would suggest that the first step for one to take in reading *Polanyian Meditations* is to enter mindbodily as fully as possible into the world which is constituted by this unfamiliar and deliberately equivocal language, as one would enter for the first time into a cubist painting.

9/27/88

All of our languages, ranging from, at one end, our body-language and gestures to, at the other, the most abstract of all languages, pure mathematics, are the instruments by means of which our conjointly present, convivial mindbodies deliver the world and themselves to themselves. One of the feats that they are required to perform in the course of doing this is to judge of the appositeness of their various languages to their several tasks, to adjudicate among them and to apprehend the logic of each of these in itself and of the logical matrices within which they jointly form a comprehension. These feats of judgment and interpretation—in our sentient appropriation of the circumambient world no less than in our most highly reflected heuristic leaps—are being performed incessantly, even though, for the most part, tacitly. Were we to become explicitly aware of them (what would prove to be an insupportable burden), we would perceive them to be prodigies that even the most sophisticated computer imaginable could not even remotely approach, because the intelligence of our mindbodies is implicated with, enformed by, and thus derivative of the logos of their biotic integrity, sentience, orientation, and motility—because it is, in short, incarnate: more exactly, mindbodily.

When the *authority* of every language without exception is thus seen to derive from the service it renders to the mindbody's relentless search for meaning, coherence, and value and could in fact have no other; and when it is seen that the privilege of a given language has been vested in it by our mutual, though tacit, assent in the intentional texture of our joint mindbodily quest, then we will see, jointly relying upon the Reality in which we primitively dwell, that in an important sense we are responsible for the reality that is made by our words to appear in our midst.

In thus acknowledging our reliance upon an unreflected Reality and in taking responsibility for our mindbodily inherence in a world which we have, in a sense, called forth, we place man back at the center of all knowing and being, thereby somewhat mitigating what Hannah Arendt has called our "twofold flight from the earth into the universe and from the world into the self."

Deprived of "presence," of an ahistorical Truth and Reality, and left with "only" history, defined as that that is destitute of access to an unchanging actuality, we are forced back upon what we take to be our altogether isolate and fleeting consciousness, adrift in the world without poise or grounding.

Our response before what to sober thought would appear to be a kind of nightmare "idealism" goes to the heart of modern ambivalence: exhilaration and nihilism. On one hand, we believe we are translucent gods, disincarnate spirits; on the other, we take this translucency and disincarnation to be the very marks of our nothingness. We are exhilarated in our nihilism and nihilistic in our exhilaration.

This is of course madness, for which modern nihilism harbors a romantic hankering because, as we think, madness, being beyond good and evil, is at least honest.

On the far side of madness lies that Being the nonexistence of which is inconceivable, that everywhere asseverates itself in all our quotidian sayings and doings, is therefore "historical" through and through, in which nevertheless the whole of our mindbodily lives are convivially grounded in the pertinacious substantiality of their pretensions and retrotensions; and so have been since time began. Under this regime Being, at once steadfast and intentional, is seen to be the provenance of reality and truth, coherence and value— closer to each of us than we are to ourselves.

Index of Names

Analytic Index of Subjects

Act: and ritual, 17; relation to ritual illustrated, 18

Acting: relation to "acting," 20–21

Anti-foundationalism: operates from within a logocentric theater of reflection, 74; cannot be said, 74. *See also* Foundationalism/anti-foundationalism

As-yet-unreflected, the: not opaque to reflection, 110

Authority, 108–9; acting on vs. justifying acting on, 108; embodied in what we are given to doing, 108

Batting a baseball: as illustrating relation of action and ritual, 18; viewed as achieving the optimum coherence in the world, 19

Being, the nonexistence of which is inconceivable: mitigates, in face of relativism, vicissitudes of interpretation, 63; asseverates itself in our quotidian doings and sayings, 63; is "historical," 63, 65; is authority for uses of 'real' and is the provenance of reality, truth, coherence, and value, 115

Cognitive act: detached analysis of, impossible, 84

Cognitive science: conditions of, for representing a cognition, 82; as reflexive phenomenology, 82; purposes of, 83; and reductionism of modern imagination, 84

Computers: disanalogies between, and humankind, 77; and sensory experience, 80–81; worldlessness of, 81–84

Computer science: aspirations of, 76; incoherence of, and philosophical anthropology, 77

Concept(s): existence of, in literate culture independent of time, 23; use of, in idealism of philosophical tradition, 27; in world of orality, 27; and usage, 68; are not "mental" entities, 69; nature of existence of, summarized, 70; to be a, to have a, 95–96; thought to be mental, 96

'Conceptual'/'empirical': sharp dichotomy between uses of, untenable, 70

Consciousness: characterized, 79–80, 103–4; nature of, as complement to philosophic conception of "rational," 103; not a faculty, 103

68; continuously fashioning coherent world, 70; as ubiquitous ground of meaning-discernment, 70; invests itself in figures of its own devising, 93; informed by logos directed toward order, meaning, rationality, and value, 111; judges appositeness of languages to their several tasks, 114

Mindbodyimage: as theory, 57

Motorscape: as theory, 57

Myth: authority of, founded in our primitive worldliness, 12, 71; thinking about, as anthropologist, 71; and memory and hope, 72; analogies between, and sensory experience, 72

Mythos/logos: opposition of, source of our existential tonus, our mindbodily oriented presence, 8, 12

Number: use of, in idealism of philosophical tradition, 27

Opposition: as the *arché* of my being, 86, 93; forms of, 86–87; subject/object as, 87

Oral/aural: phenomenology of, 28

Oral culture: and picture of concept, 29

Orality: contrasted with literacy, 101; shift from, to literacy and the obscuring of the unreflected world, 49; a phenomenology of, 87–89

Orientation to *ur*world: as condition of ratiocination, 20

Past: status of, 10; our mindbodily ensconcement in, and the future, 10; as present reality not past, 11; will have a different use applied to my existentially actual mindbody, 12. *See also* Future

Philosophical anthropology:

import for, of suppression of images of orality, 30; and subject-object dualism, 92

Philosophical tradition: less than truly radical, 25–26; and literacy, 25–26; the paradigm of value, meaning and reality of, 26; rationalism according to, 26; is "idealistic," 26; "idealism" of, abstracts us from pneumocarnal inherence in world, 31

Practical activity and reflection, 20; a phenomenology of the relation of, 20

Practice: thought to be ontologically distinct from theory, 37; defective accounts of, fail to impede, 38; the relation of theory and, in Freud, 38–40; concepts and images that form logos and telos of, are heterogeneous, 39; way in which theories bear upon, 39; and theory grounded in mindbody's sentience, motility, and orientation, 54

'Pre-history of language': meaning of, 34

'Present'/'absent': use of, in discussion of meaning of sign, 66; in contrast with 'actual'/'potential', 66–67; visualist interpretation of, 67; Derrida's sense of, 67

Primitive worldliness: as foundation of weight and authority of myth, 12

Rational: philosophic meaning of, derives from literacy values, 102; conception of consciousness complementary to, 103

'Reader': necessity of, in accounts of *différance*, 62

Reading: as inherently convivial act, 62